I Want
But I Can't

Why Our Kids Are Leaving Church

Karyn Henley

Karyn Henley Resources

I Want to Believe But I Can't: Why Our Kids Are Leaving Church
by Karyn Henley

Copyright © 2007 Karyn Henley. All rights reserved. Exclusively administered by Child Sensitive Communication, LLC.

Cover Photo: © 2007 Jupiterimages Corporation. All rights reserved. Used by permission.

Cover Layout: Ralph Henley

The dandelion logo is a registered trademark of Karyn Henley.

For permission to copy excerpts from this book, contact Karyn Henley, POB 40269, Nashville, TN 37204. office@karynhenley.com

Unless otherwise indicated all Scripture quotations are taken from the Holy Bible, New International Version®. NIV®. Copyright © 1973, 1978, 1984 by International Bible Society. Used by permission of Zondervan Publishing House. All rights reserved.

Printed in the U.S.A.

ISBN 1-933803-19-3

Table of Contents

Do You Want Me?

Do you want me to think, to ponder, to wonder –
    or do you want me to avoid the questions?
Do you want me to open my eyes
    or to close them?
Do you want me to stop my ears
    or to listen?
Do you want me to seek answers
    or to say I've found all the answers?
Do you want me to climb
    or to pretend there's no mountain?
Do you want me to sail
    or to turn away from the wind?
And if I open my eyes,
              listen,
              seek,
              climb,
              sail,

do you want me to speak

                        or to keep silent?

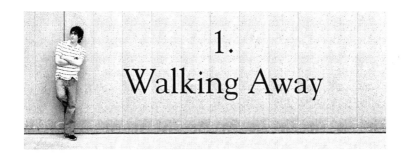

1.
Walking Away

"My son doesn't go to church anymore."

"My daughter is questioning everything she's ever been taught."

"According to my son, he's post-Christian."

"My daughter says she's a recovering Christian – like a recovering alcoholic. She doesn't want to touch 'the stuff' anymore."

I'm sure we've all heard the statistics by now: 80% to 90% of Christian young people leave church when they graduate from high school.[1] A different study indicates the same results, but states it differently: six out of eight high school grads stop attending church.[2] Other statistics show that 40% have already checked out by seventh grade, while 50% to 60% walk away in high school.[3]

This group of kids was attending our preschool Sunday School classes twelve to fifteen years ago. During those twelve to fifteen years, while they were growing up, children's ministry was also growing, getting itself enthused with all kinds of fresh ideas. We teachers learned how to help children memorize scripture and how to pay attention to kids' learning styles. We learned how to tell Bible stories more effectively with puppets, balloons, and sleight-of-hand "magic." We staged children's concerts;

we brought in new music and singing groups and performers and contagiously enthusiastic events. I know all this, because I spent those years traveling to churches and conferences, speaking to parents and teachers, and performing family concerts.

But the kids we spent so much energy on are leaving. "And the ones who are leaving were some of my best and brightest," confessed one prominent children's leader. Once our kids are free to choose, they vote with their feet and walk away. Christian ed consultant Dick Crider says they're telling us, "I sang your songs. I jumped to your music. I watched your cartoon videos. I ate your pizza. But I didn't meet your God."[4]

We tried. We were sincere. We still are. So what happened? What's happening even now? The answer is complex. And I don't consider myself an expert on the subject. But I do have some ideas that I think are worth adding to the public conversation.

It has always been easy for those of us who are parents and teachers to lay the blame on the world we live in. We shake our heads, and say, "It's the fault of our culture and the decline of values and morals in the media. We can't compete with movies and iPods and the internet." That's one way to look at the issue, and there is some validity to this stand. But, as a Chinese fortune cookie once revealed to me, "It is much easier to be critical than to be correct."

Besides, throwing a blanket of blame across society simply accuses a nebulous them out there somewhere. It's their fault. They should change. But this response leaves us overwhelmed with a sense of hopelessness gnawing at the edges of our hearts. What's more, blaming society allows us to wash our hands of all this business (except worry) and absolve ourselves of everything (except giving to groups that lobby to change *them*).

Now I'm not saying that our society has no role to play in the problem. We'll see in the next few chapters that it very definitely does. But remember what your mom used to tell you? When you point a finger at someone else, three of your own fingers point back at you.

Who is our society anyway? It's us. So it's not all *their* fault. If we don't grapple with that fact, we miss a strategic opportunity that has been handed to us on a silver platter – the opportunity to consider our part in this and do something about the only people we can truly change: us.

In other words, we need to assess ourselves and consider what we've done (or not done) in order to find out where we may have gone wrong. If we're to blame in some way, we need to own up to it and figure out how to move forward from here. Otherwise, we perpetuate our mistakes and continue to fail our kids. Remember the old adage: "Insanity consists of doing the same thing over and over, hoping for a different result." Can we afford to dig our heels in and insist on doing things the way they've always been done, just more intensely?

Listen to a few of the voices of those who are leaving the church (and they're not all eighteen to twenty-somethings; many are older). You can probably make your own list. If not, you're not listening. Here's what I'm hearing.

"I tried going to church again. But I didn't get it. What was going on? It wasn't even relevant to me at all."

"My church is a chat-room on the internet."

"Truth? It's just your opinion of what's true."

"We don't want you to tell us how it is; we want to figure it out for ourselves."

"It's weird because (Christians) are very into grace. They talk about it a lot. And mercy. They like that one too. But these are two concepts that they just never seem to be able to really apply to their everyday lives."

What are these voices really telling us? What if their church really is the internet? What if they gather daily with their community of spiritual thinkers by blog? Do they feel more enriched there than at church? Do people read and accept and comment on their blogs, while nobody listens or accepts what they have to say at church? Is church even set up to listen to the attendees, or is it set up for the attendees to listen to a few God-experts with whom everyone else is expected to agree? If someone doesn't agree, are they met with defensive posturing? Or do they feel as if they can't state their disagreement without being judged and condemned? It's time for us to ask these questions. Actually it's past time.

Let's go with some "what-ifs" for a minute. What if God wants to wake up a complacent, self-satisfied church? There are only a few ways He could get our attention quickly and effectively, guaranteed. He could fool with our financial security. He could allow our physical safety to be threatened. He could let our children shake us awake. All these things are happening – which may have nothing to do with God's plans at all. Even so, God has a way of turning things to His advantage.

Anyway, if you're willing to explore this kids-leaving-the-church issue, here's how I propose to proceed. First, we'll take a brief look at how faith develops, because the "taken-for-grantedness" of kids' faith can become a time-bomb these days.

Our second stop will be "these days" – our postmodern, pluralistic era. We'll ask why our kids might change worldviews.

Then we'll turn the spotlight on ourselves and explore some barriers we may have set up unintentionally, roadblocks that make it hard for our kids to believe.

Last of all, we'll look at what this exploration means to our parenting and to our children's ministries. In other words, what might we do about all this in practical terms?

Let me say again: I don't consider myself an expert on these issues. I'm simply inviting you to explore along with me. My hope is that we'll all emerge with a better idea of how to communicate Jesus and His love.

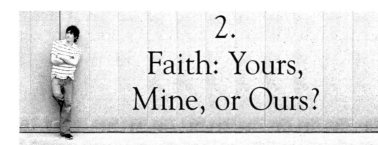

2.
Faith: Yours,
Mine, or Ours?

Classic studies in faith development show that no matter when people come to faith, they grow through stages. I've dealt with these stages in greater detail elsewhere, so I'll be brief about them here.[1]

The first stage is **imitation**. We easily see imitation in young, churched preschoolers as they mimic the signs of faith of the adults who are significant in their lives. In other words, if your toddler sees you pray with folded hands, she'll most likely pray with folded hands. If she sees you reading the Bible, you may find her one day with a book open, pretending to read the Bible, even though the book may not be a Bible.

The next stage is **identification**. Older preschoolers and early elementary kids not only imitate, but also identify with our rituals and values and other religious beliefs. This is "my church." What my church believes, I believe. What my church does, I do.

During the elementary years, a child moves into a **story-centered** faith. The child's faith is strongly attached to the stories of the community of people with whom he has identified. These include the Bible stories, of course, but they also include the examples and parables used by his community to interpret those Bible stories. Add to that the "stories" he sees as he watches his community in action. Plus the stories told by the significant people in his world about how God is working in their lives. And last, but not least, this includes the child's own stories about how God is working in his life. All these stories enrich the child's growing faith IF the telling of these types of stories is encouraged and shared. If any of these stories is missing, it doesn't mean the child's faith won't continue to grow. It just means his faith is less nourished.

Next comes the stage of **personalization**. For 'tweens and teens, the focus of life is on carving out their own identity. So it's normal for them to question their faith. "Is this Mom and Dad's faith, or is it my faith?" "Do I really believe this, or do I agree simply because my best friend or my youth pastor says I should?"

The stages of faith continue, but since our focus is on kids, we'll stop here. I want to look back at the stages now and pull out some key points that have to do with belief.

Preschoolers: Imitating and Identifying

- A preschooler will believe whatever you tell her. She believes there's a Santa Claus, an Easter Bunny, and a tooth fairy. And she believes there is a Jesus. Why? Because you told her so.

- A preschooler finds it hard to separate fantasy from reality until he's about five years old, which means he quite possibly believes that reindeer fly on Christmas Eve, while at the same time, he believes that Jesus fed

5,000 people with five loaves and two fish. The two beliefs carry equal weight.

• Preschoolers don't understand symbolism. One preschooler pointed to a lamb and said, "Is his name Worthy?" Because at church she had heard, "Worthy is the lamb."

The upshot of all this is: We may be eager for preschoolers to profess their faith and claim salvation, but we should temper our eagerness with the realization of where preschoolers are developmentally. They are gullible, and they think with preschool logic.

Two examples: One father led his three-year-old son in a prayer to ask Jesus to come into his heart. The next morning at breakfast, the boy gulped down his toast and said, "That bite hit Jesus right on the head." Another preschooler asked Jesus into her heart and then looked surprised. "It doesn't itch!" she said. When her mother asked what she meant, the little girl said, "Jesus has a beard, and I thought when he came into my heart it would itch."

Now let me make a disclaimer here. It is true that some adults who are now committed believers came to the Lord as preschoolers. I'm not saying it can't be done. God can touch preschoolers just as strongly as he touches anyone. Besides, I firmly believe that God doesn't ask us to understand everything before we choose to follow him. He didn't lay out the whole map and itinerary to Abraham. He just said, "Let's go." And Abraham went. When Peter wanted to walk to Jesus on the water, Jesus didn't explain how he was going to overcome the physics of the situation,

He just said, "Come on." And Peter came. God doesn't ask us to understand. He asks us to obey. So I don't question anyone's obedience.

What I'm trying to say is: A child's faith will most likely be a taken-for-granted faith. That faith is all he knows. It's what he's been taught. It's "just the way things are." Lesslie Newbigin, a longtime missionary to India, wrote, "In the beginning the child has simply to accept what is told on the authority of parent or teacher. There is no alternative to this. But if the parents and teachers are wise, they know that their work is not truly done until the child has reached the point where he or she can say, "Now I see for myself. . ." [2]

Elementary: Identifying and Story-Centered

- Six – Eight-Year-Olds: Kids generally still believe what we tell them (taken-for-granted faith), although they may ask some very astute and pointed why-questions. One mother was bemoaning the fact that the Lebanese were shooting rockets at the Israelis. Her seven-year-old daughter asked, "Shouldn't they shoot back? Israel shot at them first." (Which was true.)

- Nine-year-olds: Now kids look for explanations. They want to know how things work (including faith) and why things happen the way they do. They seem to focus on fairness. "And there is a growing sense that nothing is fair in the world," educator Chip Wood says of nines. "Why do children die? Why is there AIDS? Why are there poor people and how come a few people have all the money?" [3]

'Tweens and Teens: Personalizing (Or Not)

• <u>Ten-year-olds</u>: At 10, kids are still, for the most part, "actively receptive" learners. They like to talk and express themselves. They see our inconsistencies and problems, but are pretty good problem-solvers themselves.

• <u>Eleven-year-olds</u>: Now kids have an "increased ability to de-center and see the world from various perspectives." They tend to challenge beliefs and principles. Writer Randall Niles says, "When I was about eleven years old, I started asking questions about everything, including God, the Bible, and the 'meaning of life' in general. Unequipped to deliver any kind of foundational evidence, my church and family relied on the axiom, 'you've just got to have faith.' That didn't work for me."[4]

• <u>Twelve-year-olds</u>: Moody, unpredictable, hard to read. In general, this describes a twelve. They need rituals and activities that serve as a bridge or rite of passage into the adult world, says Chip Wood. They are looking for faithful friends. And they tend to argue with beliefs.

• <u>Thirteen-year-olds</u> can be touchy. They often give minimal feedback – sometimes one-word answers – to adults' questions. They may rebel against beliefs – not in the sense of revolting, but in the sense of refusing to accept beliefs. But they are interested in issues of human rights, fairness, and justice. And they are able to begin thinking about the different sides of an issue or various solutions to a problem.[5]

• Researchers used to believe that a person's brain was almost fully developed by age 13. But a recent article reported that "in the past two years, neuroscientists have discovered that parts of the brain – specifically the pre-frontal lobes, which are involved in planning and decision-making – continue to develop well into the late teens and early 20's. . . . That means millennials' brains are still developing reasoning, planning and decision-making capabilities while they are depending heavily on technology – cell phones, IM and e-mail – as well as parents and friends at the other end of the technology. As a result, some experts believe millennials struggle to make decisions independently."[6]

Notice: Our stages moved from a child who believes exactly what she's told into questioning, challenging, arguing, rebelling, and struggling to decide for herself. But that's not such a bad thing. Because in order to personalize faith, a child has to drop the taken-for-grantedness of her beliefs. So it's not unnatural for an adolescent in the midst of crafting her identity to let go of belief with one hand, only to pick it up again with the other hand. Her faith then becomes an integral part of her identity. That's the path we hope she takes.

But there are two other paths. One is the path of never questioning the taken-for-granted beliefs. This is where the time-bomb is. When adolescents move into adulthood with a taken-for-granted faith, how long will it last? When will it face serious challenge?

A friend of mine came to faith in her thirties. Recently she wondered aloud why most of the people her age at church don't seem to take their faith as seriously as she does. We figured out that most, if not all of them, had been raised in Christian homes and had gone to Christian universities. My friend and I wondered if they had ever really made the deep faith commitment my friend made. Were they still taking their beliefs for granted? Do they have reasons for their beliefs, or do they defend their faith by simply saying, "That's just the way it is"?

If we insulate ourselves in our own sub-cultural thermos, taken-for-granted beliefs may never be challenged. Of course, these days, it's harder and harder to stay insulated.

Another path an adolescent might take is dropping the taken-for-grantedness of his faith and NOT picking it back up. On this path, he does not personalize faith. Instead, he leaves faith altogether – or he leaves it in some form.

Why would a person not personalize the faith he or she has been taught? Now that we have a basic understanding of faith development, I think we're ready to tackle that question.

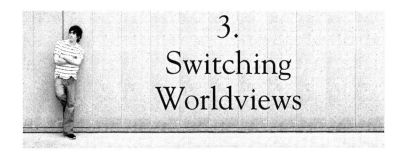

3.
Switching
Worldviews

Your worldview is your "take" on things, your perspective, the lens through which you see life. Worldview is also popularly called your "paradigm." Our question for the moment is why a person (specifically our kids) might leave one worldview or paradigm and start living according to a different one. Dr. James Hall of the University of Richmond lists three reasons that he sees for people changing paradigms.

1. Exposure to alternative worldviews.

2. Intentional culture critique or conceptual "revolution" in which people take sides.

3. Failure of their old paradigm in light of new and perplexing circumstances.[1]

Let's take a closer look at each of these from the perspective of faith.

1. Exposure to alternative worldviews.

It's an understatement to say that today we are saturated with information. The internet and other 24/7 media make different worldviews easily accessible as well as appealing. Kids can hear and see anything and everything within a few clicks. And they tend to believe the information they find. One young man reports, "New college grads strongly believe all Internet information is valid, and if it's not available on the Internet, then it doesn't exist."[2] If that's true for college grads, I'd say it's true of teens and younger kids as well.

So maybe we should be grateful for kids who are skeptical and question everything. In an information-saturated age, it's healthy to be skeptical. It's just that we start worrying when they're skeptical about what they've been taught about God.

Yet one of the things our kids are discovering is that the United States is not a Christian nation. It's a pluralistic nation. That means different religious beliefs and teachers co-exist. As a society, we're expected to tolerate, respect, and give equal rights to the wide variety of beliefs around us. Most of our kids are exposed to these different beliefs and worldviews through friends, neighbors, teammates, and co-workers, who often live by very different religious and philosophical paradigms.

So why might someone change worldviews? Because another worldview looks better somehow. It's different and intriguing. Or it's more comfortable and accepting. Or it seems, in some way, to be right.

2. Intentional culture critique or conceptual "revolution" in which people take sides.

Our culture critique and conceptual "revolution" began in the 1960's and '70's, when we started shifting from modernity to postmodernity. Historically speaking, you might say it was about time for such a change to occur. Modernity began in Europe with the Renaissance (1300's) and included the Age of Reason and the growth of science, humanism, and technology. One source points out that toward the end of modernity, a shorter, more intense, even extreme, period of modern thought reigned: *modernism* (World War I through the 1950's). In the 1960's, the pendulum sailed the other direction into a short (1960's until around 2000), intense, extreme period of postmodern thought called postmodern*ism*.[3]

Modernity (Modernism------------)	(Postmodernism----------	Postmodernity->
1300's 1920's – 1950's	1960's – about 2000	from 1960's – ?

Today, there's talk about post-postmodernism. What to call this emerging era is under debate. Suggestions include Performatism, the Age of Synthesis, a Trans-(fill-in-the-blank) age. Whatever it ends up being called, it's still part of postmodernity, but it's moderated somewhat from what was espoused in the last half of the 20th century. Many of postmodernity's most radical elements (postmodernism) have been questioned and left behind by philosophers, which is good news.

But this is not a return to modernity – which, frankly, is also good news. The bad news is: The kids we're talking about in this book grew up in the short, intense, radical period of postmodernism, and the prevailing winds are still full of turbulent postmodern paradigms.

The fallout of all this is that we and our kids are thoroughly engulfed in a postmodern world. The rest of this chapter will explore exactly what that means and what it has to do with faith. I think once we see what's been happening – to us as well as to our kids – we'll understand better how the church got to this crossroads. And maybe then we can see more clearly the most promising path to take from here.

So let's take a brief look at postmodernity. Earlier I used the image of a thermos to represent an insulated subculture. Now picture dozens of thermoses, each representing a different culture, lined up on a table. Each thermos contains its own traditions, beliefs, values, and language. (Even in cultures that share a language, the various subcultures use language in tradition-specific ways to communicate their beliefs and values.) Postmodernity gets its start with this simple fact: Each person is brought up according to the particular worldview of a specific culture.

That's pretty much a no-brainer. If you're brought up in a Jewish household, your worldview will be Jewish. If you're raised in a Catholic household, you'll have a Catholic paradigm. If you've been brought up Buddhist, your outlook will be based on Buddhist principles. Okay, so what's the big deal?

Communication, for one thing. Take the simple statement, "God loves you." If I say, "God loves you" to a group of Christians, who share my paradigm, I know everyone understands me. By "God," we mean a personal, loving deity who exists as Father, Son, and Holy Spirit. When I say "loves," I don't mean sexual love or the "I-love-chocolate" kind of love or even a friendship kind of love. I mean the "I'll-give-my-life-for-you" kind of heroic, self-sacrificial, other-centered love. And when I say "you," I mean you as an individual. You understand me if you come from my paradigm.

But if I tell a group of Buddhists, "God loves you," they hear something very different. First of all, they don't have a god. Their highest power is an impersonal force. Second, their view of "love" falls into the category of "desire," and desire causes suffering, which is what they are trying to escape. So love is not something good. Third, there is no such thing as "you." "You" as an individual do not exist. You are simply a part of the one whole soul which comprises the cosmos.

Even if we speak the same language, our starting point for discussion (what we take to be a "given") may not be the same. A liberal starts with the presumption that change is inherently good. A conservative starts with the presumption that change is not inherently good.[4] So they can argue past each other forever if they don't look for common ground somewhere.

It's not only our language and our unstated presumptions that hinder communication. Dr. Robert Solomon points out that "rituals can seem ludicrous if you're not part of them."[5] From the Christian worldview, we scratch our heads at some of the rituals of Buddhism, Hinduism, and other religions. But then, other religions can be just as puzzled over Christian rituals. In a postmodern context, "religions look less like expressions of religious experience and more like social practices which give shape to individual experience," says Phillip Carey of Eastern College.[6] In other words, instead of religious practice expressing your worldview, it appears that religious practice creates your worldview.

Anyway, out of this different-cultures, different-languages viewpoint (notice how it overlaps with pluralism), postmodernity arose and began questioning the motives of modernity. Modernity had promised that progress, fueled by science and reason, would answer all the world's ills. But postmoderns began to point out that rational thought and "progress" led to oppression, wars, and the destruction of our environment.

Postmodernity says, "Enough already," making a move that's not so much a shift as a backlash against modernity. (By the way, this focus on oppression has spawned a sense of victimization. So another effect of postmodernity is that all of us tend to see ourselves as victims of someone else's power play – drug companies, mortgage lenders, deceitful politicians, religious leaders, and so on.)

Here's a brief contrast of the differences between modernity and postmodernity:

Modernity Values	Postmodernity Values
- rationalism	- mysticism
- intellect	- intuition
- science	- spirituality
- dogma	- experience
- nationalism	- globalism
- individualism	- community
- capitalism	- environmentalism
- segmented life	- holistic life
- character	- image
- focus on the future	- focus on the now
- absolute truth	- relative truth

The last point is perhaps most disturbing for Christians. It's postmodernity's dilemma, the "collapse of truth," as N.T. Wright puts it.[7] Postmodernity says each culture, along with its own language and rituals, has its own values, its own "rights" and "wrongs." So what's right for you may not be right for me; what's wrong for you may not be wrong for me. And what's true for you may not be true for me. In other words, there is no absolute truth. (Of course, that's stated as an absolute truth. Go figure.)

An absolute standard is seen as a "Tool of the Oppressor." Tradition appears to be manipulation and control. Truth claims are judged simply to be power-plays, agendas to get whatever the claimant wants. What this means is that when the Bible is held out to postmoderns, they don't ask, "What is the truth which is here articulated? but What is the interest which is here being advanced?"[8]

Now, it's not as if our children are handed a list of postmodern positions they can mull over, and then they can check off the ones they want to own. No, the way this works is that these views gradually drift through society, year by year, generation by generation, until they saturate the societal air we breathe day and night. So while we are raising our children to pray and memorize scripture and worship, our children – and we ourselves – are breathing postmodern air. We can't not breathe.

Those of you who are younger may not even see what the big deal is. Those of you who are older may be saying, "Not my kids." Or "This is just typical, temporary generation-gap stuff." But some of you know that, yes, it is your kids. And no, it's not temporary. While there may be some generation-gap stuff in it, it's a major societal cyclone. It's already blown through, and "Toto, we're not in Kansas anymore."

To be specific, we're talking about the millenial generation, today's 8 to 29 year-olds. "This group, also called Generation Y and the Net Generation, is made up of 80 million people in the United States born between 1978 and 1999," reports Kathryn Tyler. "They are the first generation to use e-mail, instant messaging (IM) and cell phones since childhood and adolescence."[9] So they stay connected to media and technology. Which means they're getting lots of their advice from whoever's on the other end. Friends. Moms and Dads. Music. It's all about input.

Yet all that connection can and is often accomplished in isolation. While friends and family and music and blogs are reachable wherever and whenever with very little effort, input providers are, after all, at the other end of the connection. And when the call is ended or the earbuds are taken out, there's often no one there. This is a lonely generation. Disillusioned. Cynical. With very little hope for the future. A friend of mine, Joseph Watson, works almost exclusively with postmoderns for Youth With a Mission (YWAM). He says, "They're orphans, hungry and scared, with no identity. All their thoughts are on surviving."

Many postmoderns survive by consuming (which someone once defined as "knowing the price of everything and the true value of nothing"). They're into "credit card religion, retail therapy, brand consciousness," says Carl Tinnion, also with YWAM.[10] But before we wag our fingers at postmoderns too many more times, let's be honest.

How many of us are caught up in the same things? After all, we're breathing this air too.

In fact, Tinnion warns us not to look at postmoderns "as the nadir of civilization." Instead, he encourages us to discover how we can "speak their language and confront their empty worldview with truth."[11] In this truth-denying age, there may be only one Way that offers absolute Truth. In a purposeless, hopeless age, there may be only one Way to find purpose and hope. In an age starved for faithful, unconditional love, there may be only one Way that offers true Love. And in the life of a postmodern who secretly yearns for truth, purpose, hope, and unconditional love, yours may be the only voice offering it. The question is how to make your voice clear and credible. I hope that by the end of this book, you'll have an answer to that question.

Let's review for a minute before we go on. We've been looking at why young people might change paradigms or worldviews.

1. Exposure to alternative worldviews. (Pluralism.)

2. Intentional culture critique or conceptual "revolution" in which people take sides. (Postmodernity.)

Let's go now to one more important reason – one that has to do with how well we are preparing our children not just to survive, but to thrive in a pluralistic, postmodern world.

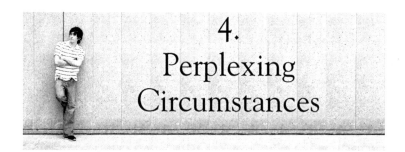

4.
Perplexing
Circumstances

"Much damage will be done if we are not vigilant. It has already been done, in our failure sufficiently to arm our young people and prepare them . . . and in our slowness to realize the need to supplement our old apologetic, directed against a Modernist foe who has long been passe." Dr. Donald Williams, professor and pastor, gave this warning at a recent commencement address.[1] He was talking about postmodernity and the church's failure to prepare our kids to deal with it. When kids aren't prepared, they discover the third reason for changing their worldview:

3. Failure of their old paradigm in light of new and perplexing circumstances.

Postmoderns place a high value on experience. They believe what they can see and touch, feel and hear. When they've been taught to believe one thing (their taken-for-granted paradigm), but they experience something different, then they find themselves perplexed. To tell you the truth, I do too. What are we to think when there's a dissonance between our belief and our experience?

For example, many of our kids are raised to believe that anyone who's not a Christian is a loser – sinful, decadent, foolish, and miserable. But lots of non-Christians are kinder, more giving, more altruistic, and more accepting than many Christians. In addition, the non-Christians seem happier! So what happens when a Christian kid discovers that many of her friends hold values higher than hers and are more dedicated to their non-Christian religion than her fellow-Christians are to Christianity? At that point, there's a dissonance between belief and experience.

A high school grad from our church went off to college in Chicago to study pediatrics. When she came home for a break at the end of the first semester, she said she'd made a lot of friends, most of whom were not Christians. But she said she felt more respected, encouraged, and "at home" with this group of friends than she felt with any group at church. Wasn't it supposed to be the other way around? Her old paradigm and her new circumstances were clashing.

According to many postmoderns, the old paradigm dispenses irrelevant information at church and doesn't address them "where they live." One young man, a Christian, came out of a church service shaking his head, saying, "I don't get it." There was a dissonance between what he heard at church and what he experienced in everyday life.

Postmoderns have a reverence for the mystery of the spiritual. Someone once said, "Life's not a puzzle to be solved but a mystery to be experienced." That's a very postmodern way of looking at it. In contrast, as novelist Flannery O'Connor pointed out, the modernist notion held that "the aim of learning is to eliminate all mystery."[2] A belief that the Bible (or the pastor or the Sunday school teacher) should eliminate all mystery is dissonant with the experience of being hungry for spirituality. Missionary Lesslie Newbigin wrote,

" . . . if the supreme reality is a personal God whose we are and to whom we are responsible, then there is something quite absurd about the posture of those who claim infallible certainty about God in their own right and on the strength of their own rational powers. In our interpersonal relations, we would never make such a claim for our knowledge of another person. How absurd to make such a claim with respect to God!"[3]

After all, who in the world is more mysterious than God? But, if a spiritually hungry Christian keeps getting pat explanations of God at church, she may turn elsewhere. Maybe to the blog world. Maybe to religions like Buddhism and Taoism.

With mystery comes awe and reverence. In our attempts to show God as an accessible Father, loving and caring, maybe we've made Him too familiar, too common, too trite. Remember when the disciples were in a storm on the sea with Jesus, and He calmed the wind and the waves? "The disciples just sat there in awe. 'Who is this?' they asked themselves."[4] Maybe our prayers should contain more "Who are You?" awe.

Our kids also sense a dissonance when we feel free to critique ("judge" or "condemn") everyone else, yet we get all bent out of shape if anyone tries to critique us. Postmodern critical inquiry is often called "deconstruction," which means taking apart traditional, "taken-for-granted" concepts – architecture or health issues, sexuality or politics, business or religion or whatever. We take it apart and evaluate each piece as to whether it fits or works in our lives. Then we throw out what doesn't work and keep what does.

But remember the thermoses? Insulated Christianity is often not open to critique. Not even from within. We are known as stubborn, arrogant people who think we know all the answers. We're viewed as people who get aggressive or defensive when we're challenged, and who insist that even non-believers live according to our beliefs.

To look at it from a different angle, we set ourselves up as those who have all the answers, yet our answers often sound canned, recycled, cliche. They don't sound like they come from our deepest beliefs, but from doctrinal statements to which we've given assent. Kids sense a dissonance when we claim to be passionate about Christ, yet the phrases we use sound suspiciously like echoes of the latest popular Christian writer or speaker.

When our kids offer challenging questions and comments, but our responses don't measure up, they feel the dissonance. Listed below are some types of responses that dodge honest, open discussion. Are we guilty of any of the following?

1. Side-stepping the question

We side-step by saying things like, "Well, he's a Muslim. Of course he'd say that. He's just deceived." This type of response is not an answer; instead, it shifts the focus onto a different subject.

2. Borrowing our beliefs

A friend of mine who does mission work in Europe was at a gathering of Christian young people there. As he passed a couple of young men, he overheard one say to the other, "See that guy over there? He's going to hell, because he smokes." My friend paused and asked, "What makes you say that?" The young man answered, "Go ask my pastor. He'll tell you why." If only someone else can explain why you believe something, then you have a borrowed belief.

3. Relying on bandwagon beliefs

"No one in our church believes that." Or "No true Christian would consider such a thing." This type of answer implies that we are all in the same wagon, so we all think alike. Maybe bandwagon beliefs and borrowed beliefs used to work, but not anymore. In a postmodern, pluralistic society, "we are now in a situation where we have to take personal responsibility for our beliefs," writes Lesslie Newbigin[5].

4. Following tradition blindly

As in: "We've always done it that way." But note the word *blindly*. There are traditions worth keeping. Which means we choose to keep these traditions, because they hold some meaning, some significance for us.

5. Using emotional reasoning

When we react to kids' questions and comments with fear, distress, or anger, we're using emotional reasoning, which usually short-circuits any meaningful conversation.

6. Falling into circular reasoning or faulty reasoning

Circular reasoning would be something like:

"Why do you believe the Bible?"

"Because it's God's word."

"Why do you believe it's God's word?"

"Because the Bible says so."

"But why do you believe the Bible?"

This reasoning can start over again from the first sentence and circle around ad infinitum; plus, the thing you're trying to prove is also used as the proof, which proves nothing.

An example of faulty reasoning is what the U.S. Deputy Under-Secretary of Defense for Intelligence used in 2003 when he told an audience how he defeated a Somalian Muslim fighter: "You know what I knew – that my God was bigger than his. I knew that my God was a real God, and his was an idol."[6] If that statement is true, what about Christians who get killed by Muslims and others? Does that mean their god is stronger – or that their God is the true God – in that situation?

7. Holding some beliefs as untouchable [7]

This is the "Don't-even-go-there" response. We don't question our beliefs or allow anyone else to question them. We practically hang out a sign: "Closed to discussion." Ruth Tucker, associate professor of missiology at Calvin Theological Seminary, has interviewed many former Christians who are now atheists. She says, ". . . where tough questions are silenced – here faith-threatening doubts often emerge."[8]

None of these lines of reasoning satisfy wondering minds, nor do they respect the questions, so they don't respect the one who asks the questions. In addition, these types of responses unfairly place the answerer in the superior position. They don't add any real, plausible ideas to the search, nor do they allow for mystery or admit that the answerer may be just as puzzled as the questioner.

In short, these responses frustrate the goal of critical discussion and leave our kids on their own with the same questions they had in the first place. Kids soon realize that their parents and teachers, the very ones who claim to be teaching the most important beliefs in the world, can't handle inquiry about those beliefs. Kids are left with a sense of dissonance.

I'm not pointing out all this in order to heap guilt on our shoulders or to mock our good efforts. But sometimes we don't see our mistakes, because they're masked by all our good intentions. When I write, I get so close to the subject and the words on the page that I need another reader to find mistakes I don't see and to question sections that aren't expressed clearly. My hope is that by pointing out some specifics, we'll be able to do more than just wring our hands about our kids.

In one of Jesus' last prayers, He said, "I'm not asking you (Father) to take them (my followers) out of the world, but to keep them safe from the evil one. . . . I am sending them into the world. . . . I am praying not only for these disciples but also for all who will ever believe in me because of their testimony."[9]

We're supposed to go out into the world. And there's no doubt that most of our kids are doing just that.

The question is: Are we sending them out prepared? Do their beliefs stand firm when they experience the world, or do our kids discover a dissonance between what they've been taught to believe and what they experience?

I'm not talking about the dissonance we all feel between godliness and sin. That will always exist. But if God is truly God and His love is truly the supreme love for all, then God and His love will be appropriate for any type of world we live in. Our kids should not see their beliefs as dissonant, but as exactly what their experiences are calling for. Yet that doesn't seem to be what's happening. Something is obviously out of sync somewhere.

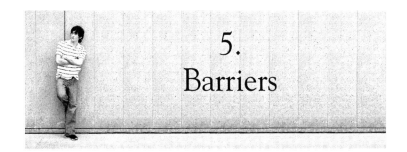

5.
Barriers

"Dear God,

I do not have an easy relationship to you, God. I am confused by your press. I have read so much about you, from so many quarrelsome experts, that I do not know who you are – IF you are. . . . Where should I begin? I like your world. . . . Perhaps we agree on that. Who knows? Maybe we agree on my gripe about 'God experts,' too. They make it feel so hard to know you."

- Julia Cameron[1]

Jesus said that He's the Good Shepherd and that His sheep follow Him because they know His voice. If our kids are leaving the church, maybe they don't know the voice of the Good Shepherd. Maybe what they hear from us is not His voice, but the voice of "God experts."

Have we made it hard for our kids to know God? Have we unintentionally set up barriers that keep them from a living, growing faith? If so, what might some of these barriers be? We've touched on a few already: failure to allow for the mystery of God, posing as those who know all the answers, fallacies in reasoning. Could it be that we need to change the way we do things, the way we talk, the way we think, in order to connect with postmoderns?

Ruth Tucker says, "We need to look at ourselves and ask what it is about the gospel, about our own testimony, about our faith community, that is not appealing. I need to ask what is unattractive about me as a Christian in my faith community." She quotes author Walker Percy as saying, "It's a mystery: If the good news is true, why is not one pleased to hear it?"[2]

Good question. Why are our kids not interested? Maybe we've set up barriers. Roadblocks. Like what? Maybe . . .

Hypocrisy

"This is one of the reasons why the Christian religion has lost so much credibility. Many contemporaries can no longer take it seriously. They meet religious men and women who are not authentic and who seem egocentric because they are obviously pursuing their own goals, while they cultivate a pious jargon, as if they cared about nothing but God and his kingdom." So say writers Richard Rohr and Andreas Ebert.[3]

Hypocrisy, of course, is not a new roadblock, but that doesn't make it any less lethal to faith development. As one teacher points out, "If there is no objective difference between gold and iron pyrite, people are not going to commit themselves to serious prospecting."[4]

False Gods

What? We believe and teach the one true God. How could a Christian have a false God?

Easy. Simply worship something besides God. Make something else the hub of your life. We can quickly point to lifestyle issues and say that sports could be our god, or movies, or money, or shopping, or . . . we could go on and on. And it's true that if our kids see us trusting these for our security, then what we espouse as our beliefs will show up in dissonance to how we live. Hypocrisy again.

But let's dig a little deeper and look at issues we might not have thought about. What about:

• <u>The Bible.</u> Could the Bible be a false God?

Missionary Jacob Loewen says, "Religiously, God is made in the image of our particular biblical interpretation. We see our own understanding of God as biblical, that of other Christians as not."[5] The Bible can become our God if we make it, instead of God, the hub of our lives.

We say the Bible contains Truth. But is the Bible God? Truth was around long before there was a Bible. Did Abraham have a Bible? Did he know Truth? Did Jacob and Joseph read a Bible? Did they know Truth? If during the night tonight, all the Bibles in the world disappeared, would Truth disappear?

Truth is not WHAT. Truth is WHO. Truth is GOD.

Ken Rideout, missionary to Thailand, says, "Scripture is not true simply because it is in the Bible. On the contrary, it is in the Bible because it is Truth."[6] There's a big difference.

• <u>Church.</u> Could the church be a false God? Listen again to Jacob Loewen.

"For some people, some groups, some denominations, the specialized God of religion has begotten a son, a junior God, the church – my denomination, my community of believers. . . . When the church is God, the community of those who hold common beliefs and practices and who submit to a common rule becomes the ultimate object of trust and loyalty. The church becomes the source of truth. What the church teaches is believed and is believed because it is what the church teaches. The church is trusted to be the judge of what is right and wrong and the guarantor of salvation.

"When the church is God, to have faith in God is to have faith in the church. To turn to God is to be converted to the church . . . The way to God is through the church. . .   God is defined as the one in whom the church believes." [7]

Notice Loewen's definition of who or what is our God: "the ultimate object of trust and loyalty." What else might be the hub of our lives, our object of trust and loyalty?

• Rituals. We can subsitute rituals for God. Show up for church. Read your Bible every day. Memorize scripture. All of these things are good. But that's why it's so hard to recognize and dethrone a Christian false god. Do we place our ultimate trust in our Christian rituals? Are they the hub of our lives? Or are they a response to the One at the hub?

• **<u>Worship.</u>** We can worship worship if we make it the hub of our lives. Is our worship focused on us or on God? Are our prayers about God or to God? Do we sing primarily about God – or to God?

• **<u>Doctrine.</u>** When we camp around peripheral issues, do our positions speak louder than the Shepherd's voice? Jesus said, "By this all men will know that you are my disciples," . . . if you proclaim doctrines loud and clear so all the world can hear? They will "know that you are my disciples," . . . if you gather to protest the politics and movies you don't agree with? They will "know that you are my disciples," . . . how? Love.

Wait, wait! you say – there's nothing wrong with protesting what we believe to be wrong policies or immoral media. That's not my point. My point is that our doctrines are not God. But they can become a false god if we center our lives around them, and if the world – and our kids – see our protests and not our love.

We're known as people who protest often and loudly over issues that offend us, while we neglect getting actively involved in issues of justice that are obvious to even non-Christians: poverty, race, the environment, education. Our kids want to see us actively addressing injustice for the betterment of the world, not just to win converts.

To sum up, when we set ANYTHING above God, who is Love, Christianity will ring false.

The Corporation

"'Religion' has kept more people from God than anything else in history," says former atheist Randall Niles. "Following Jesus is not about the man-made machine we know today as 'Christianity.'"[8] A friend of mine says church is not institutional correctness, it's the people. He says the group approach no longer works; our community should be built around the work of Jesus, joining Jesus in His mission – and His mission is not to "have church" but to lift humankind.

So the question is: Are we corporate Christianity instead of a vibrant, relational community? Are we teaching and preaching and conducting our "church" affairs as though we're marketing Jesus to consumers? Are we marketing the Bible? the church? God? Are the attendees simply consumers? Tim Stafford says, "Churchgoers infected with consumerism understand church not as a gathering of God's people, but as a program offering. Consciously or not, they look for the church that targets their market profile – their musical tastes, their worship style, their age, race and income level."[9]

One problem with marketing to consumers is that marketing is often hype. Half-truths. Not too long ago, I went to the web-page of a Christian ministry. Across the page was a slogan similar to this:

"Bringing up creative kids in an uncreative world."

My first impulse was to join the hurrah and say, "Yes! We're bringing up creative kids in . . ." *Wait a minute,* nudged a little voice. *Look again.* I did. And I realized the slogan wasn't true. The world is not uncreative. Some of the most creative people you'll find are not in church.

So what happens when we go around spouting untruths or half-truths as if they were rallying cries? What happens if our kids buy into a slogan like this, only to realize later that the meaning is iffy at best? Should we be surprised if they decide we were less than honest with them? Should we wonder why they question the truth of whatever else we've told them?

Gimmicks are another questionable tactic. A recent article in *Children's Ministry* magazine reports, "Many preteens find biblical matters irrelevant. Why? Because much of Bible learning is rooted in gimmicks. The Bible? Useful for a prize. Scripture memory? Earn a badge. Attendance? Score a gold star. And when bribes no longer bait, as happens with many preteens, they yawn and walk. Once the test's complete, the exodus begins."[10]

Besides, if we're marketing Christianity, we're in trouble. Researcher Juliet Schor writes, "Today's consumers are equipped with a cynical mental radar."[11] Postmoderns are cynical anyway. Why push them further?

Postmoderns are agenda-shy. They can smell an agenda a mile away. You yourself probably cringe when you sense that someone is talking with you because they have an agenda instead of wanting to converse as a friend. Has the church become an agenda-driven corporation, competing among other corporations for attention? Is that why we're losing?

And we are losing. Stastistician George Barna has pointed out that the church is not even close to being a significant influence on our society. Another report shows that many of our culture's leaders "find churches irrelevant as they attempt to express meaningful faith in daily life." [12]

The Greenhouse

Bob Hope, scheduled to speak at a college graduation ceremony, was asked to give his advice on going out into the world. "My advice?" he said. "Don't go."[13]

Do we isolate and insulate our kids and ourselves in a greenhouse atmosphere? A Reader's Digest article from 2005 predicted trends for the next 10 years. One was the growth of the market for Christian products. "It's reached a point where Christians have come close to creating an entire parallel universe in which, from the first sip of morning coffee from a 'Go God' mug to an evening soak in Dead Sea Bath Salts, it is possible to choose an explicitly religious alternative for almost every imaginable product, service and form of entertainment."[14] What a nice, comfortable thermos we live in!

On the other hand, has thermos-living given us a "we vs. they" warfare mentality? One Christian father told me how proud he was of his son, because when he was playing soccer with his friends, another boy used a bad word, and his son said, "I can't play with you anymore." And his son left the game.

It made me wonder: Do we Christians look at the world and say, "We can't play with you, because you use bad words (or whatever)." Now this, of course, calls for wisdom, especially in what we expose our children to, and when. But my point is that we should watch our attitudes. Why are we surprised when the world acts like the world? When we're with non-Christians, they often feel that we look down on them as if they're second-class citizens.

"We're in, you're out."

"We're saved. You're lost."

"We're wise. You're foolish."

"We're good. You're bad."

"We're right. You're wrong."

One former Christian, now an atheist, said that one of the best things about becoming an atheist was that he no longer felt the spiritual superiority he used to have when he was with non-Christians.

Have we perceived or implied that people of other beliefs are bad people? Have we taught an across-the-board condemnation of all other religions? Missionary Ken Rideout points out that after fifty years under Communism, the Chinese are some of the most loving people in the world. Maybe we should start asking what people of other religions do right and start from there.

When our kids see us isolate our Christianity in a greenhouse and condemn everyone else, they are not impressed. Postmoderns want to treat non-Christians as spiritual peers. That might not be such a bad idea. After all, we're all created in God's image, and we're all searching for the same thing, though we may not know it.

Abandonment

The millenial generation has been labeled with many terms. One of the most heart-breaking is "children of abandonment."[15] Yet when I look back at the past twelve to fifteen years and ask what went wrong at church, I can't help but acknowledge that one of our major problems during that time was the difficulty we had recruiting Sunday School teachers. It has been practically impossible to get a teacher to commit to an entire year. So we've compromised. Our pleas of "give us six months" changed to "give us one quarter," which changed to "give us one month," and then "trade off with someone else – teach every other Sunday for a quarter." By and large, parents have remained uninvolved, and teachers have pulled back until they, too, are uninvolved in the lives of their students.

Have we, then, formed programs instead of relationships? Teachers often go into the classroom with the goal of teaching the material. We should be going into the classroom not primarily to teach the material, but to teach the kids. To get to know them. To build relationships. The Irish poet William Butler Yeats said, "Education is not the filling of a pail, but the lighting of a fire." Sometimes it's easier and faster to fill the bucket than to rub flint and create a spark.

Have we been unwilling to pay the price to meet our kids' needs? Do we even know what our kids' needs are? Have we spent enough time with them? Have we listened to them? Have we found out what they do well? Have we encouraged them in their strengths, their dreams, their visions? Do we really care?

Burn-Out

This barrier is most common among the kids of pastors and church leaders, because often "there is no distinguishing line between home and church."[16] But burn-out can happen to the children of any highly dedicated Christian family or any over-controlling church. Are we over-scheduling, over-programming our kids with "Christian" activities? Does everything they do have to relate to the church? Are we swamping them with everything Bible so that eventually nothing in the real world seems relevant to their lives and nothing in their lives seems relevant to the real world? Are they burning out?

"Here is the test of any presentation of religion," writes William Barclay. "Does it make it wings to lift a man up, or a deadweight to drag him down? Does it make it a joy or a depression? Is a man helped by his religion or is he haunted by it? Does it carry him, or has he to carry it? Whenever religion becomes a depressing affair of burdens and prohibitions, it ceases to be true religion."[17]

Division

One of my husband's colleagues calls herself a recovering Baptist. She doesn't go to church anymore, even though she still believes in Jesus. Her opinion is that one reason so many people are leaving church is because they're tired of being taught to hate other people. Including other Christians. They're tired of drawing lines – within Christendom – to separate who's in from who's out. They just want to follow Jesus. They want to love the Lord and love their neighbors.

One study indicates that if young adults don't think the church they attend is helping them become more Christlike (loving), they'll leave and look for a church that will – even if it's a home group or a blog or a network of friends who meet at Starbucks.[18] I know of young people who are embarrassed to go by the name "Christian" anymore. They're not ashamed of Jesus, they're ashamed of the church. Some of them are truly searching for another name to call themselves. One young couple says simply, "We follow the teachings of Jesus."

These are the young people who "get it." They've been able to sift out the sand of the denominational claims and intra-church squabbles and hold onto the gold nugget, the greatest commandment of Love, the one by which we're to be identified. Other kids don't stick around. If Christians can't even agree among themselves, how should our kids know whose doctrine is right and whose is wrong? And why should they care? They've got better things to do.

A few months ago, I made a list of some of the issues over which Christians disagree. The list included:

death penalty

Jews

the Bible — inerrant   evolution
— literal
— figurative
6-day creation
theistic evolution
millenialism   baptism
premillennialism
amillennialism
the Kingdom
demons - yes? no?

hell — forever
— for a time
war — annihilation
church and state
spiritual gifts
predestination

That's not an exhaustive list (although just thinking about it is pretty exhausting). But it was enough to set me pondering. Bible scholars have studied these issues backwards and forwards. But they don't all agree. Could Jesus have made all these issues perfectly clear? Could God have straightforwardly explained each one? Of course. Then why didn't He? I can think of only one answer: Something very important transcends all these issues. Love. And God wanted us to put Love into play where all these issues, and others, are concerned. That's the only way to have unity.

I'm not saying we're not to have opinions on these issues or that we're not to express our opinions from time to time. And those opinions may be strong beliefs. But we tend to get on bandwagons and tell people that taking a certain stand on one or more of these issues is what it means to be Christian. I think Jesus didn't make all these issues crystal clear because He wanted us to have to supercede all of them with love. It's the narrow way, but it leads to life. The other way leads to destruction. Of each other! Then there's the collateral damage it causes for our children and for the rest of the world, who won't touch our boxing ring with a ten foot pole.

Heaven Focus

Have you ever heard the saying, "He's so heavenly minded, he's no earthly good"? Does that describe the church our kids know? Get your ticket to heaven now, then you can take a seat and breathe easy. Just make sure you don't get off the train before it reaches its final destination.

But the way we sometimes describe heaven – is it a place our kids want to go? After a "season" at our church in which a lot of emphasis was placed on the second coming of Christ, one young man moaned, "I don't want Jesus to come back yet. There are lots of things I want to do. I want to grow up first."

A friend and I were swapping stories about how our separate congregations were being encouraged much the same way by different worship leaders. With dreamy expressions on their faces, these worship leaders excitedly told our congregations to just think about it – one day we'll all be in heaven before God's throne, worshiping day and night forever and ever, singing and making music before God. "Frankly," said my friend, "that sounds more like hell to me." Of course, it's heaven to musicians and music-lovers who can think of nothing more fulfilling than singing and playing their instruments here on earth – or in heaven.

But as N.T. Wright says, the church "does not exist to provide a safe haven in which people can hide from the wicked world and ensure that they themselves arrive safely at an otherworldly destination." Instead, he says, we are "called to be agents of God's healing love, putting the world to rights."[19]

One godly friend and mentor said he believes one reason people unplug and reject us is that they have a social conscience – for race, poverty, women, and the environment – and Christianity is seen as doing little, if anything, to light these dark places.

So is Christianity all about being saved for the afterlife? I propose that Christianity is all about being loved perfectly. Being saved is a subset of that love. Once we've experienced God's life-giving love ourselves, we get to extend His reign of love by learning and practicing that same kind of love toward everyone we meet.

Those are the barriers I've identified. There may be more. Did you get defensive reading about any of them? We recoil the quickest when someone touches a sore spot. So I'd suggest taking a closer look at how those particular issues play out in your life and in the lives of your kids or your church group.

Now I know you'd never intentionally set up any barriers to keep anyone, especially our kids, from coming to Jesus or staying the course. I also know that not every parent or teacher is guilty of setting up these barriers. My sole purpose in pointing them out is to get us to take a look at the critique being given to us by our kids. Are they right? If they are right, and if we don't change, will we end up being simply "noisy gongs and clanging cymbals" with nobody listening?

When God called Jeremiah, He said Jeremiah was "to uproot and tear down, . . . to build and to plant."[20] In my neighborhood, there's a lot of new construction going on. Small, old, one-story houses are being torn down, and spacious, new multi-story houses are being built on those lots. The uprooting and tearing down is done in order to clear the land so the new can be built and planted. That's what we may need to do. What do we need to tear down? How can we build?

I have one more barrier to mention. I saved it for last, because it will transition us into practical ways to address the needs and views of our postmodern kids.

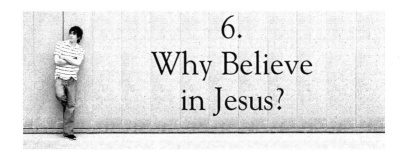

6.
Why Believe
in Jesus?

Failure to Teach Why

We've taught kids what – Bible facts and stories. We've taught kids how – how to worship, how to memorize, how to be a Christian. But have we taught them why it makes sense to believe in Jesus (other than "you'll go to hell if you don't")? Have we helped them develop a faith that can be explained simply, a faith that will stand firm when they're challenged by our pluralistic, postmodern culture?

Maybe the reason we haven't concentrated on the "why" is because we can't explain it ourselves. Do we know why we're Christians?

If you've read some of my other books that deal with apologetics (the "why" of your belief), then this chapter will be a review for you. I include it for those of you who've not encountered this fresh way of explaining why you believe in Jesus. I was exposed to this way of thinking by the friend I mentioned earlier, Ken Rideout. Ken was a missionary in Thailand for 44 years. He often had to explain the why of Christianity to people of an Eastern mind-set, which happens to be the same mind-set that now permeates our own postmodern society.

Let's start with why you believe. Answer the following questions:

- Do you truly believe that Jesus is God's Son?

- Do you believe Jesus lived on the earth, never sinning, but living a perfectly holy life?

- Do you believe He died on a cross and rose from death by the power of the Holy Spirit?

- Do you believe He is the living Lord, reigning today and bringing salvation and the hope of eternal life?

- Do you truly believe all this?

- Why? Prove it.

Let me up the ante:

Prove it without using the Bible.

What? Not use the Bible? Why go this route? Because of two groups of kids. First, the kids who are leaving the church in droves. They've been brought up hearing scripture. They've been inundated with it. They know what you're going to say, and they're not impressed. It's as if they're immune to it.

The other group is non-Christian kids who will challenge your own kids about their faith. Non-Christians expect us to use the Bible as proof for what we believe, because the Bible is the Christian holy book. Muslims go by the Qur'an. Taoists use the Tao. Buddhists have their writings. Hindus have the Vedas and Upanishads. So why should a non-Christian value the Bible's teaching over the Tao or any other religion's scriptures?

So . . . can you prove what you believe without using the Bible? Remember, Truth is not what, but Who. I assume, then, that your faith is not simply an assent to a set of beliefs, but trust in a Person.

Let's try another set of questions:

• Is it right for me to murder you?

• Is it right for me to steal from you?

• Is it right for me to abuse you in any way?

All humans, Christian or non-Christian, will answer those questions the same way. These are truths humans just know. More questions:

> • If I love you perfectly, will I murder you or steal from you or abuse you? (All people answer the same way.)

> • Does anyone love you perfectly?

> • Do you love perfectly?

> • Does anyone in the world love perfectly?

All people answer the same way. You see, we all know that someone who loves us perfectly will be kind, will encourage us, will share with us, etc. A knowledge of what perfect love is, has been programmed into all humans. Not that any of us love perfectly. In fact, that's where we all fail to live up to this inner standard. And we all know it.

We also know that what goes around comes around. What we plant, we reap. So when we mess up, we know we deserve to be paid back in full. In many religions the ultimate payback is hell, either temporary or permanent. In some religions, there's samsara, a cycle of reincarnation in which your future life is payback for the life you're living now. Life-death-life-death-life-death, on and on and on until you merit a release from this cycle. The whole focus of these religions is to get out of the cycle.

Even an atheist knows that no matter how hard she tries, she keeps creating her own little hells in the back alleys of her life. No matter what religion or philosophy, no one can love perfectly.

• Now, if there is a God, is He greater or less than you?

• What is the best attitude you can have toward another human being? (It's what we just said all people know about: perfect, unconditional love.)

• So if there's a God, isn't He at least as great as this best attitude of yours?

• Is Love personal or impersonal? (Can a pencil love you? Can a light bulb love you?)

• So if God is Love, is He a thing (an impersonal force) or a person (a Living Being)?

God is Love. He is personal. That's why we all sense this love as a standard within us. Because we're persons made in His image.

• So is this standard for God to live up to or for humans to live up to?

We sense that this standard is for us to live up to, yet we know only God can live up to it. But that doesn't seem fair. Is God, then, just watching all of us try and try again until we ultimately fail? Does that sound like perfect love?

• What is the greatest act of love that one human can do for another?

Novelists and screenwriters know the answer. The greatest thing one person can do for another is self-sacrifice. You see it in great movies and novels all the time. So if God wants to show humans how much He loves them, how must He do it?

Perfect Love (God) MUST become human,
born under the system of payback,
to do for humans what humans can't do for themselves
(love perfectly and take the payback for our bad choices),
so that humans, destined to make hells of our lives
can instead find true, purposeful life.

N.T. Wright explains this beautifully: As a human, Jesus lives for us and shows us just how much He loves us by drawing the evil of the world – political, social, and emotional evil – like poison to Himself and dying from it. [1]

This apologetic begins at a different place than most others. Most defenses of the Christian faith start with trying to explain the validity of the Bible or the reality of the death and resurrection of Jesus. But try starting with the incarnation – why God had to become human.[2] Do you understand that message? Do you feel it? Can you communicate it without using a Bible?

Once you see why God had to incarnate, it's easy to believe His resurrection. And it's easy to move into the Bible. Because if God came to earth as a man, what do you think He'd do? Probably heal sick people, feed the hungry, right wrongs, teach with great wisdom, show us how to love. That's exactly what you see in the Bible.

I'm not saying you have to memorize this approach. I don't think you should use it as an agenda. I am saying that this is why I believe in Jesus. The important thing is that if you work with kids, you should know why YOU believe.

But be careful. Think. One teacher said she explains why she believes by pointing to the night sky. All those stars, the orderly operation of the universe, its beauty. How could you not believe? It's fine for her to confirm her own faith that way. But is it convincing to someone else? Plenty of people who look at the stars and study the sky remain atheist. The sky might inspire me to believe there's a God (or gods), but it definitely doesn't tell me that God became human – nor does it tell me why.

So as you contemplate why you believe, look at it from the point of view of a non-believer, or a kid who's just dropped the "taken-for-grantedness" of his beliefs, or a postmodern who says, "That may be true for you, but it's not true for me." Can you tell him why you believe in such a way that his spirit knows intuitively that it's true?

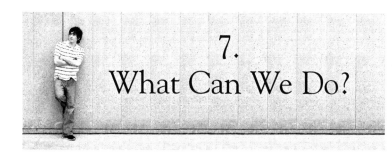

7.
What Can We Do?

Since our shins are still stinging from bumping into so many barriers, we can readily see that the obvious answer to "What can we do?" is "Remove the barriers." Of course, that's easier said than done. You may recognize barriers that those in key church positions don't even see. You may start dismantling a barrier only to have someone else nail it back in place. On this road, the church as an organization is an oversized eighteen-wheeler. It takes a long time for one of those big rigs to make a tight U-turn. By contrast, you're a sportscar. As an individual, you can turn much faster. So how do you do that?

Here's the problem in a nutshell, summed up by Lesslie Newbigin, who writes from the perspective of a British citizen. Britain has been pluralistic a lot longer than the U.S. Newbigin says, "The problem of communicating (the gospel) in a pluralist society is that it simply disappears into the undifferentiated ocean of information. It represents one opinion among millions of others."[1]

So how do we communicate our message? Let's start with the messenger. What is it that's burning so strongly in your heart that you have to communicate it to kids? Please don't answer, "That they're going to hell unless they repent." Is that the best we can do? I'm asking what we have to offer them – and I think the answer is something a little better than a fire insurance policy. Especially for pluralistic postmoderns who are NOW focused, not future-focused.

What, then, from their perspective, do you have to offer?

A harbor for one thing. A safe haven. When the seas get choppy and downright dangerous, there's nothing like catching a glimpse of a stable mooring you can steer toward. That safe haven is Jesus as He shows up in us.

As parents and teachers, we have a faith that's still active and growing, so we ourselves will continue to question and explore how God's love plays out in our own lives. But we're confident that it does. And we're unwavering in looking to Him as the purpose and meaning of it all. We're certain that God's plan of love furnishes us with the tools we need to cope with the ups and downs of life. So whatever happens with our kids, it helps them if we remain stable – not stubborn and closed, but stable.

But does our harbor look safe, inviting? Or would kids rather risk the rough seas?

Professor Peter Jacobi advises writers to "Be aware of your readers' wants."[2] Maybe we need to be more aware of what postmodern kids want. YWAM's Joseph Watson says we're not answering the questions these kids are asking. They want to know:

1) Who am I?

2) Why am I here?

The only people they trust to help them answer those questions are people who care enough to spend time with them and listen to them. Maybe we don't know what they want, because we're not listening. Before He taught, Jesus took 30 years to listen and understand as a human in the midst of normal human experience. So surely we can take some time to listen. That's part of what we're up to in this book. So then, if we're listening, what's the next step?

Michael Larsen, a literary agent, says, "For a medium of communication to become integrated into our lives, it has to be usable in the four B's: bed, bath, beach, and bus." [3] What can we offer kids that they can take anywhere? Maybe we can offer the clues to Who am I and why am I here. So, fellow-messenger, maybe that's our doorway in.

Let's zoom out for a minute now and look at our postmodern children's faith-growth as a whole. If we focus our message on Who am I and why am I here, what will the message look like to kids of different ages?

In general, the answer to the two key questions is embedded in two Bible verses. The first is, "Love the Lord with all your heart, soul, mind, and strength, and love your neighbor as yourself" (Mark 12:30). The second verse shows how we are empowered to love: "We love, because He first loved us" (1 John 4:19).

As I line this message out, I'll put it in terms of Who am I and why am I here. I'll also follow the educational path of introducing, deepening, and maintaining. Note: The following addresses only the message. It's not an abbreviated Sunday school scope-and-sequence. We'll look at models of communicating the message in a minute.

Preschool: Imitating and Identifying with Faith

In preschool, we introduce all these concepts in a variety of ways. As we repeat the message, we deepen and maintain it.

Who am I? I am:
- one God made
- one God loves
- one God cares for

Why am I here?
- to let God love and care for me
- to love God back
- to enjoy God's creation and thank Him for it
- to love and care for what God has made, including other people
  This includes basic cause and effect: my choices and their consequences.

Elementary: Identifying with Faith and Story-Centered Faith

Notice how the concepts introduced in the previous stage are deepened and maintained, and new concepts are introduced.

Who am I? I am:
- one loved by God
- one God made and gifted for a purpose
- one who can't live up to God's Standard (Perfect Love)
- one for whom God became human, lived, died, and rose again

- one given freedom to choose whether or not to be a son or daughter of God

Why am I here?

- to love God and get to know Him better
- to develop habits that will help me know God
- to discover how God helps me cope with any situation
- to learn and practice other-centered love (Genesis 12:2)
- to use my gifts to perpetuate love, goodness, beauty (God's character)
- to be a friend to others
  Include learning about other religions. Explore cause and effect; moral choices; what makes something right or wrong. Explore the concept of self-sacrifice. Use stories, examples.

'Tweens and Teens: Personalizing Faith

The basics are being maintained and deepened, and new challenges are being introduced.

Who Am I? I am:

- one loved by God, made and gifted for a purpose. What is your purpose? How can you find out? Are non-Christians gifted by God?
- one who can't live up to God's Standard (Perfect Love) How far does this Standard go? How do you know what's right and wrong? Wrestle with the dilemmas of perfect love in an imperfect world.

- one for whom God became human, lived, died, and rose again. How do I know this is true?
- one given freedom to choose. I can be a son/daughter of God or I can be a spiritual orphan. What are my options? Why would I choose Christianity?

Why Am I Here?

- to love God and get to know Him better
- to develop habits that will help me know God
- to discover how God helps me cope with any situation
- to learn and practice other-centered love (Genesis 12:2)
- to be a friend to others – include learning about other religions
  Incorporate multi-cultural sensitivity and respect.
  Explore cause and effect; moral choices; what makes something right or wrong.
  Consider and embrace self-sacrifice. Use stories, examples.
- to use my gifts to perpetuate love, goodness, beauty (God's character)
  Explore character vs. image.
  Individuate and integrate faith into every day life, including concerns about environment, equality, justice, poverty, etc.
  My life is my project. I get to choose the type of person I want to be. What life

habits should I cultivate that will set me
on that track?

I tossed in a few challenging questions/directions
above. It's best if kids can raise these – and other – questions themselves. But if they don't, you may find it worth-
while to prime the pump. And remember that kids sometimes need to talk things out so they can hear themselves
think.

In addition, kids sometimes start out by making
statements and taking stands they think you'll disagree
with. This is part of individuating. What they're trying to
say is, "I can think for myself and come to my own con-
clusions, different from yours." This is where your respect
and patience will earn great rewards. If you continue to
ask probing questions and to listen, consider, and take seriously their discussion of their specific issues, they will
trust you and be more likely to speak their hearts and listen
to yours when the time comes.

What I did not include above is the specific actions
to take. Kids don't want to just discuss. They want to act.
They need to be involved in real-life opportunities to feed
the hungry, serve the elderly, and clean up the environment
with mentors who can help them help others and reveal
God's life-giving love. Which brings us to the next topic.

The Sunday School Dilemma

One caveat to the above chart: It could all be bundled
into business-as-usual unless we come at it creatively from a
postmodern angle. In other words, our most effective
ministry in this new age may not be in the old wineskins.

I'm sure someone more creative than I (and more post-modern) can come up with creative new ways to communicate the message more effectively. Meanwhile, I'll give you my opinion on our old options.

• Worst way to communicate with children: Children's church.

• Questionable: Sunday school.

• Worst Sunday school situation: Teachers changing from week to week or month to month, or using DVD's as the primary teacher. (Note: "products do not love us back." [4])

• Good Sunday school situation: One or more teachers (at least the lead teacher) stays with the children for at least a nine-month stint.

• Best Sunday school situation: One or more teachers start with the kids when they're preschoolers and graduate with them, moving with the group through all grade levels.

• Even better: Small community groups or house groups with members committed to each other; apprentice-type or mentor-type relationships between those young in faith and those more seasoned in faith.

• Best: A family working together, playing together, listening and loving. This is a type of apprentice or mentor relationship

Why am I evaluating our wineskins like this? For a couple of reasons. First, we are no longer a one-size-fits-all society. "When we cookie cut," says Joseph Watson, "we run the risk of repelling people." In-and-out teachers don't really get to know the kids who gather with them for a couple of hours once or twice a week. In that case, the kids are usually viewed as a group and managed as a group.

What's more, whatever curricula teachers use, they need to be creative in their thinking and in their metaphors. The best metaphors come from knowing the kids and what touches their lives. It's not that kids can't be influenced for good by in-and-out teachers during a large group time. And maybe it's the best we can do. But it's not the optimum situation. So maybe we shouldn't be surprised if it doesn't give us the optimum result.

The second reason I'm less than jazzed about today's Sunday school paradigm is that there are only two ways I know to communicate: modeling and discussing (which includes listening as well as speaking). And the most effective modeling/discussing is done by living, breathing, caring humans one-on-one or in small groups. Why? Personal relationship.

If you're going to train someone to take over your position at work, how is it best done? It helps if, at first, they follow you around, watching and listening and asking questions as you do the job. But it's not long before you ask them to help you do it. Then you ask them to do the job, with you as the helper. Then you watch them do it on their own. It's personal. It's active. It's involved. They get to ask questions, even suggest how things might be done better.

Modernity propagated top-down hierarchy. Postmoderns are all about synergistic relationships. Even leaders are most effective if they're seen as part of the team. It's about community.

But church is a community, isn't it? So why are our kids turning their backs on our church community? Think again. Church is a community? Usually not. A gathering of individuals in one location to go through their sacred rituals does not make a community. It simply makes a temporary collection of individuals all doing the same thing at the same time. Do people sit in church and check their watches, looking forward to the final Amen so they can leave and go join their community? These days, they may sit in church and text-message the people in their community.

The community postmoderns are looking for is found in personal friendships. That's why if we want to do a better job in Sunday schools, we need people committed to being there consistently, developing relationships, nurturing faith. Families need the same thing. Helping kids grow a living faith in a loving God takes time. It's a process.

So if you want to be the influential person to one kid or to a whole group, you'll have to care about kids individually. It's like being a mentor. Ask them questions about themselves. They love for you to talk about them, listen to them, and consider what they have to say. They want you to take them seriously.

I know this is not a quick-fix answer. It requires time that most people don't have. It calls for a commitment that many are not willing to make. And it presupposes a gracious, open, listening heart that a lot of us have never practiced with our kids.

But do you see the opportunity here? What new direction might God have for His church in the coming years?

Agent Michael Larsen tells an interesting story about New York City. "At the end of the nineteenth century, shortly before the building of the first subway, New Yorkers believed that the city could never grow to a million people, because there wouldn't be enough room to stall the horses." [5]

Maybe God has in mind something for which you and I don't even have the context to dream or imagine.

8.
Practical Postmodern Specifics

As far as I can tell, there are three threads to weave into our dealings with postmoderns. We've touched on them already, but I want to unravel each one a little farther.

1. Personal relationship
2. Purpose for life
3. Principles for a healthy worldview

1. Personal relationship

Emphasizing personal relationships may be a way of going back to the way it was in early Christianity. Ben Witherington III, professor at Asbury Theological Seminary, points out, "Christianity was not in the first instance a movement generated by texts, but rather one generated by oral proclamation in a largely oral culture and by the making of personal contacts and the building of personal relationships – the creating of community." [1]

Oral proclamation in the first century came in tandem with a lived life. In other words, you don't talk it 'til you're living it. Remember, postmoderns are into experience. The more they experience your love, mercy, and faithfulness, the more credible you become. Author and blogger Christian Crumlish points out, "Authority is something that will emerge gradually from a dialogue and a record of one's past statements . . . Credibility will no longer be handed down with credentials." [2] That's good news. You don't have to hold an MDiv degree or be a PhD to have authority. But you do have to be found trustworthy.

At first, your attempts at friendship may be met with postmodern skepticism and the cynical suspicion that you have an agenda. (Do you? You must earn your way to their heart, and you don't do that with a religious agenda. As an older friend of mine said, "They can smell religion a mile away, and they want nothing to do with it.") To disarm that skepticism and suspicion, you'll need to be authentic and credible: You've been transformed by your faith in Jesus, but you don't forget where you came from. You admit your past and present struggles. You are transparent. You extend mercy and grace.

Dr. James Hall reminds us that "relationship does not have so much to do with a catalogue of propositions or list of theses" as much as "I believe in you and I am committed to you." [3] That's the same way our witness unfolds, not by propositions, but by commitment to a person.

Musician/pastor Rob Frazier says the modern era's notion of witnessing was, "Here's a book (the Bible). Read it and assent to its teachings." With postmoderns, you first ask about them – with true interest. And when it comes to witnessing, you make your personal confession. So, for example, instead of arguing scriptures, Rob says, "I went through some really tough times – similar to what it sounds like you're going through. Questioning. Confused." As he goes on with his personal story, he comes to a place where he says, "All I can say is I'm changed. Once I was that way, now I'm this way. And when I read the Bible, the Holy Spirit speaks to me. The words jump off the page."

That's Rob's way to get at the message. And it's a good model. But because relationships are flexible, there's no one way. That's why listening is crucial – listening to your friend and listening to the Holy Spirit. Carl Tinnion suggests asking God to show you the context in which the message will best communicate to the person (kids or young adults). That's the key, says Joseph Watson. "Lord, give me the analogies and stories that will touch this person's life." He says, "Use stories. You can teach brilliant points for hours and it won't work, or tell a five-minute story, and it will hook them."

2. Purpose for Life

Joseph connects with postmoderns through their yearning for belonging and purpose. He showed me a large simulated diamond in a velvet pouch, which he carries around in his pocket. When he gets into a discussion with postmoderns, he asks what their dreams are for their lives. He shows them the diamond and says that those dreams are one facet of God in them. He talks about how God has placed those dreams, those yearnings, those giftings within them. They are unique. Their life has purpose. They are valuable.

You can see how Joseph is touching the Who Am I? and Why Am I Here? questions. He wants kids to see that their destiny is not a what-I-do question, but a question of who they're becoming. It's about being, not doing. "What you do is not who you are," he points out. "But when you're in the world, what-you-do is all you have as your identity."

Joseph's "diamond" is something meaningful to him. With it, he can communicate the message authentically from his heart: "Let me tell you who I am, where I'm going, what means something to me."

So the context you choose will have to be something meaningful to you.

Pocket Stories

What Joseph is doing is presenting what I call a "pocket story." When I taught preschoolers, I quickly came to understand the need to have a few stories "in my pocket" for those moments when it wasn't quite time for the next activity. The purpose of Joseph's story is different, but the principle of having stories "in your pocket" is the same. And, as Joseph said, by telling a story, you can connect much quicker than you could if you tried to teach a brilliant point. Besides, there's a great precedent for storytelling: Jesus used spur-of-the-moment stories all the time.

The stories you tell can be something you heard that meant a lot to you, or they can be your own personal stories. Here's one I've used:

My older son is a film maker. One night he and a friend worked late in our basement, creating set pieces. They left the basement door open, because they were going in and out of the house a lot. About two in the morning, they stopped work and locked the door. The next morning, I got up and began making the bed upstairs. Then I noticed two eyes peering up at me from the shadows beside the bed. It was a cat. But it was not our cat. I talked softly as I reached down to pick up the cat, but it hissed and scratched at me.

So I withdrew, went to the kitchen, and returned with a handful of cat food. I tried to coax the cat out, but it wouldn't come.

Once again, I went to the kitchen. This time, I came back with a broom. I asked my son to open the front door so I could shoo the cat out. But the cat, terrified, jumped into the windowsill and began trying to climb the windowshade.

Now there was a window right next to the one the cat was in, so I opened it, thinking the cat would jump right out. Instead, the cat cowered in the first window, then clawed and climbed. All the while, his way out was only a few inches away from him. At last he saw his escape route and shot out the window.

It made me think about us and God. Why do we hiss and claw at the One who is trying to save our lives? Why do we freak out over the One who only wants to show us the way to escape our terrifying circumstances? Why do we back ourselves into a corner trying to run from God?

Another idea is to have "pocket sayings." One I like is: "Play it forward." In other words, let the past be the past. Start fresh and go forward from here. It's a maxim that encourages me and, I hope, encourages others as well.

You can see that my story and saying are not for all occasions. They have to be told in the appropriate context.

Even then, these stories may not strike you. Maybe they won't touch the person you have in mind. (If you know that, it means you're listening.) But I'm sure you have stories and sayings that mean something to you. That's the key. What stories and sayings has God used to encourage you? And what does your friend need at this moment?

3. Principles for a Healthy Worldview

Literary agent Donald Maass contrasts modernity's "mandate to accept ourselves the way we are" with the "postmodern dream of becoming something different." He says postmoderns are seeking "deep down, soul-shaking irreversible transformation for good and for always." [4]

Peter Jacobi puts it beautifully. He says he wants to find, "Belief at a time so much else works to destroy it. Faith in an age when whirlwinds of confusion rip at my consciousness. Feeling in a world that numbs us with too much information and the emptiness of advertising or promotion-driven experiences. Assurance, in an era of doubt, that verities and qualities still exist. No, not merely that they still exist, but that they can have an impact and cause me to smile or to weep or to thrill." [5]

In a waterless desert, a traveler values and longs for water. In the same way, when absolute truth is denied, there's a corresponding yearning for absolute Truth. When meaning and purpose are no longer considered part of the cosmos, there's a corresponding longing for meaning and purpose. When traditions and beliefs are being deconstructed all around us, there's a corresponding longing for a solid foundation and framework for life. When spokespeople for a purely postmodern society take down the signposts that point to morality, there's a corresponding need among life's travelers for moral direction.

All that spells opportunity for those of us who are deemed trustworthy by a postmodern friend. If we aspire to help postmoderns find the belief and assurance Peter Jacobi talks about, we need to be ready to challenge them to confront the distortions in the postmodern worldview. To show them the water in the desert, we may need to first help them see just how dry that desert is.

We're going to toss around a few of the common postmodern views and counter them with challenging questions and ideas. But first, a few helpful hints from Joseph Watson:

1. Don't use words or phrases distinct to biblical Christianity. When kids are cynical and burned out on church, "Bible-speak" and "stained-glass-window words" turn them off, and they can't hear the message for the words.

2. Use the Bible as support rather than proof. Remember, it's not true because it's in the Bible; it's in the Bible because it's true.

3. Ask probing questions to help kids see their thinking and the weakness of their beliefs.

4. Expect obstacles and doubts. Newbigin reminds us, ". . . we must have the courage to make statements that can be doubted." [6]

5. Expose the troubling implications of postmodernism.

What kinds of probing questions? What do we need to know in order to challenge postmodern thinking?

Let's go back to some of the beliefs that our society has bought into, beliefs that have trickled into the thinking of many of our kids, and perhaps into us as well.

Culture and Language

It's true that each of us is a product of our culture and upbringing. It's also true that we should respect people's beliefs and traditions. But does that mean all cultures and traditions are equally effective in making "contact with a reality beyond the human mind"?[7] We might ask, "What cultures seem to most effectively address our human condition – and why?" [8] Lesslie Newbigin points out that, unlike Christianity, other religions "illustrate the unchanging human condition but make no claim to change it irreversibly." [9]

It's also true that each subculture speaks a different language or may interpret the same words differently. But does that mean we share no communication whatsoever with people of other cultures? Are there no commonalities that transcend language?

Besides, what words do you use to speak of feelings and concepts beyond description, beyond language, beyond your total grasp? What language does the heart speak? What are the words that truly describe hope or joy or love?

Have we moved our discussion now toward a shared yearning that links humans with something or Someone that transcends the human? Even the famous atheist Bertrand Russell admitted, "The center of me is always and eternally a terrible pain – a wild pain – a searching for something beyond what the world contains." [10]

Is this a yearning for something or Someone who is not completely comprehensible or expressible?

The apostle Paul's prayer in Ephesians was that we will experience the length, width, height, and depth of God's love, even though we will never understand it. In the Paradiso in the Divine Comedy, Dante finds himself unable to put his heavenly vision into words. As Cook and Herzman point out, "He becomes part of what he sees: He does not understand; he experiences."[11]

Could this inexpressible experience be the language God uses most often to speak to all humans? I'm not necessarily referring to dreams and heavenly visions like Dante had, although it would include that. But how about the inexpressible experience of a newborn wrapping her tiny hand around your finger. Or the awe of viewing a hidden valley lake from a mountain pass. Or catching a succulent scent on the breeze. Or savoring an exquisite flavor. Or hearing music that makes you want to dance – or fly.

So instead of focusing on cultural differences, perhaps we'd be happier and healthier if we found our common ground and shared the language of the spirit.

Truth claims.

As I said earlier, the statement that "there is no absolute truth" is itself a statement of absolute truth. So it's a self-defeating statement.

But what if you truly believe there's no absolute truth? Where does that lead? What are the ultimate consequences?

For one thing, it leads to questioning everything. Every statement is shaky. Everything can be questioned.

Everything's fair game. Even Darwin? Yep. Atheism's statement that there's no God? Yep. Everything is meaningless. Even the act of questioning. If there's no truth, there's no answer to any question. So why bother to ask?

Which worldview seems to be the healthier one: there is truth, or there is no truth? Which leads to hope? Which makes you want to get up in the morning and make something of your life?

One reminder: If we are really going to hitch ourselves to absolute Truth, it helps to realize that Truth is not what, not a set of propositions. Truth is Who. Truth transcends time and space. Truth has always been and always will be. Truth leads to life and perfect, other-centered love. [12]

Atheism

The voices of atheism are growing louder and louder these days. Atheists are missionaries on a mission to convince us and our kids that we don't need a god. But I wonder why they're so insistent on their mission. "You don't try to refute something you don't take seriously," says Professor Thomas Noble.[13] So why would atheists take God-believers so seriously? One reason is that they see us as a threat. They point to all the religious wars, the abuse of religious power, the fanaticism that even today is oppressing and terrifying people in the name of spiritual beliefs.

We certainly can't deny that religion has abused and oppressed. But so has atheism. Nazism. Marxism. Communism. And long before Christianity, the ancient world wiped out each others' tribes on a regular basis. It seems to me that the problem is not God. The problem is people.

At least Christianity teaches us to love our enemies and do good to those who mistreat us. It's a religion of grace and mercy, forgiveness and reconciliation. When Christians oppress and abuse, they are not following the teachings of Jesus. When atheists oppress and abuse, it's the outworking of their no-absolute-truth, no-standard-of-perfect-love philosophy.

Other atheists say that the suffering in the world proves to them that there's no such thing as a loving God. So how do you as a Christian answer that? If you just shrug your shoulders, it might be time for you to ponder the issue. I've dealt with it in another book, so I won't go into it here. But if you're interested in looking at how various people through the ages have handled this question, you might want to read *If God is Good, Why Do We Suffer?* I also highly recommend a book by David Marshall that challenges a variety of atheistic claims: *The Truth Behind the New Atheism*.[14]

Disillusionment

Postmoderns are a daycare generation. Many are latchkey kids. Most moms and dads work. Many postmoderns come from single-parent families or blended families. Who made promises to them? Who broke the promises? Who kept the promises?

Plus, these kids grew up on tv, videos and DVD's, CD's and iPods, computers and all kinds of digital games. Which are all illusions of reality. Remember: "Products can't love you back."

But if illusion is not reality, and you get dis-illusioned, maybe that's not so bad. We don't get bent all out of shape because the sun "rising" is an illusion. We accept it and live with it. We don't get depressed because the moon "shining" is an illusion. We understand it and deal with it.

So you thought your parents were supposed to love you perfectly (i.e. to be God)? Now you're dis-illusioned. Good. Start building a healthier, more realistic relationship with them.

So you thought the church was full of people who treated everyone like Jesus treated everyone? Now you're dis-illusioned. Good. Start accepting flawed humans as flawed humans and give others the grace you want them to give you.

If you're dis-illusioned, you have the opportunity to start coping with reality, which is a lot healthier than living under illusions. What, then, is reality? Is there any meaning in life? If there is, where do we find it? That gets back to the "Who am I and why am I here?" that we discussed above.

The Bible as an Agenda

Postmoderns may argue that the Bible is just someone's agenda, a power play. But that criticism can be deconstructed with the same argument: "Accusing the Bible of being an agenda may be simply your power play, your agenda."

The Bible, says N.T. Wright, is not like any other 'holy book.' The Bible invites the reader to become a fresh character in the story. [15] It summons us to make the biblical world verifiable by the way we live. In other words, as

Professor Luke Timothy Johnson points out, when we believe that humans are created in God's image, we can't oppress or abuse them. If we believe others have infinite worth and treat them that way, then we make the biblical world a verifiable world.[16] God transforms our lives, and we exhibit that unconditional, other-centered love that the Spirit confirms as Truth in the hearts of all humans.

Maybe we should suggest to postmoderns that they read the Bible not with an eye toward culling out propositions, but toward a perceptual understanding. What do we perceive in the story, in the writings? Do we not perceive a Being outside time and visible space who is operating within the confines of time in each historical age? Do we not perceive that this Being is giving us the clues we need to operate in both dimensions ourselves? Do we not see that He has made us His embassy here within time and space? Do we not see His mercy and love reigning supreme?

Maybe we should take the personal question, "Who am I and why am I here?" and place it in Jesus' mouth. Picture Jesus asking you, "Who am I and why am I here?" What an intriguing question to have as your guide as you read through the Bible. In fact, that question is, in essence, the same one Jesus put to His followers when He asked, "Who do you say I am?" When Peter answered, " You're the Christ, the Son of the living God," Jesus said Peter didn't think of that answer because of physical evidence, but because of a spiritual realization. God's Holy Spirit verifies to the human spirit the truth of who Jesus is.[17] Peter had an "Aha" moment. So can we.

Sin

These days the word *sin* is solely a religious word.
But all in the world it means is "missing the mark." It's
like an archer shooting an arrow at a target. The "mark" is
the bull's eye. Or in basketball, the "mark" is the basket.
Spiritually speaking, what's our "mark?" It's the Standard
of Perfect Love (God). When we don't love other people
perfectly, we miss the mark. When they don't love us perfectly, they miss the mark.

Jesus told us a simple way to remember where the
mark is in practical terms. I think of it as the DiTtO rule:
Do To Others as you would have them do to you. Treat
other people the way you want to be treated. Respect.
Love. When we don't treat others that way, we miss the
mark. We sin.

But Joseph Watson stresses that with postmoderns,
you can't just give a rule. You have to explain why. (By
the way, that's the best way to raise morally savvy kids in
the first place. Tell them why you're asking them to
behave a certain way so that when you're not around to
enforce the rules, they'll know the reason for enforcing it
in themselves.) Anyway, as you work with postmoderns,
ask them about the consequences of this or that choice.
Get them to think about cause and effect long term – the
fruits of their decisions. Joseph says it's more helpful to
talk about the fruit of the sin, not the sin itself.

One of the problems postmoderns have is discern-
ing right from wrong. That's not surprising for kids
who've been breathing the air of no-absolute-truth. They
even have a different way of looking at reality.
Postmoderns "do not view knowledge as a matter of 'get-

ting reality right.'" says Josh McDowell. "They seek instead to acquire habits of action for coping with reality." [18]

Okay, so let's approach it that way. What kind of person do you want to be? Who do you admire? Why? Who do you respect? Why?

The Dalai Lama is much-admired these days. He's seen as a symbol of peace and calm. But you might point out what Dr. Robert Solomon notes: The Dalai Lama "practices such techniques as prayer, meditation, and so on; the habit of using these techniques has established in him a personality in which anger, resentment, hatred, and envy are nonexistent." Solomon goes on to suggest that we ask, "What kind of habits can I establish to make myself a different kind of person?" [19]

So we might ask postmoderns, "Is there anything you admire about Jesus? Anything you'd want to emulate about His life? Why or why not? What habits might take you that direction? Prayer? Meditation on Jesus' teaching? Bible reading? Gathering with other Jesus-followers?

Even with good habits, though, the problem is that no one in any religion is 100% faithful to his or her faith. Not even the Dalai Lama. The question is, "What happens when you're not faithful?" The world has no way to cope with that reality. Choose a religion; pick your form of condemnation.

We humans know there are consequences to our choices. We can pretend we didn't ruin certain parts of our lives and relationships, but we did ruin them. We can pretend it's okay, but it's not okay. Something's still "rotten in Denmark" to paraphrase Hamlet's Marcellus. [20]

BUT, the beauty of God's life-giving love is that He knew we were going to mess up – because we're not God, which God knows, of course. So God took care of it. In Jesus, there is no condemnation. Even our sins and failures now spur us to love, to have mercy and compassion on others who can no more overcome their sin than we can overcome ours.

Hope

A world without God is a world in which we are born, grow up, grow old, get sick, and die. One event follows another in meaningless progression. There's no source of it all, no purpose, no destination. Some atheists say that makes them value each moment of life, each human being as precious, because this is all there is. It makes them treasure what they have. They've made their own meaning out of a meaningless situation.

But atheists are in the same boat with the religions we talked about earlier. They can describe the human condition but can do nothing to transform it irreversibly. In their case, hope is little more than wishful thinking that they're leaving the human condition better off than they found it.

But true hope is confidence. Confidence in Perfect Love, who has a plan and a purpose that will never be thwarted. Of course, if there is no absolute Truth, then there is nothing to place such confidence in.

Why would your postmodern friend want to place confidence in Jesus? Maybe because Jesus first proves Himself trustworthy to your friend. Maybe you invite your friend just to try Jesus and see. One of Jesus' first invitations (to a couple of guys who would later be his followers) was, "Come and see." So maybe our invitation should be, "Try Jesus. He's not going to twist your arm to follow Him. If He's not faithful to you, you're free to look elsewhere."

There are two elements to notice in this invitation. One is that we're not inviting our friend to follow some wise teacher who has long since died. We're inviting our friend to enter a relationship with God who has lived in human form and is still alive. The second element is that we're inviting our friend to belong to a circle of friends before coming into a full belief.

Can they belong before they believe? I think they already do. Jesus' death was for all. He bought their freedom from condemnation long ago. Maybe all they need to do now is "come and see. See what God offers." Flannery O'Connor said it this way: "If you feel you can't believe, you must at least do this: keep an open mind. Keep it open toward faith, keep wanting it, keep asking for it, and leave the rest to God." [21]

As we have occasion to reiterate God's offer, we might encourage kids to look at what God has handed them: Himself. You have an older brother who, when you are faithless, He remains faithful (2 Timothy 2:13). You have One who always speaks up for you in God's presence (Romans 8:34).

You have a Creator who has a purpose for your life and is intimately interested in what you do and in the health of who you become. Jesus pointed out that God sees every sparrow that "falls" (which William Barclay says probably means in Aramaic, "light or hop on the ground"). So, says

89

Jesus, if God cares so much for the sparrow, how much more does He care for you? "No nation ever had such a conception of the detailed care of God for his creation," writes Barclay. [22]   He says, "All non-Christian religions think of a demanding God; only Christianity tells of a God who is more ready to give than we are to ask." [23]

Jesus demands no rites or rituals. The only work He asks is to believe (John 6:29). The only rule He gives is to love (Matthew 22:38, 39). So with Jesus, our life goal becomes very simple: Learn and practice love.

Are we being soft on people to say this? Tim Stafford questions evangelism that "tries to make commitment as easy as possible." [24]   I question it too. But notice: I said our goal becomes simple. I didn't say easy. The path of other-centered love is a journey in which we can invest our lives. Learning and practicing God's life-giving love is the most challenging task ever offered to anyone. But embedded in the task is the mercy necessary for failing at it. With God's life-giving love, when we fail, we can get up and try again with no condemnation hanging over us.

We – and our kids – can always fall back on love. Unconditional, other-centered love. Life-giving love. Self-sacrificial love. This kind of love crosses all boundaries – modern, postmodern, post-postmodern, whatever was or is or is to come. Love is appropriate for any age, any era. And love is . . . relationship.

So it gets back to Personal Relationship. This time, with God. Ultimately, God is offering relationship with Himself. In human relationships, we place faith in a person based on his or her character. Our faith in God is based on His faithfulness and reliability. We trust in a Person who is Trustworthy.

Modern evangelism was "interruption marketing." But in an age of "do not call" lists, evangelism is based on

1) Living a life of other-centered love
2) Being an authentic friend
3) Telling the story of your relationship to God.

"In your hearts set apart Christ as Lord. Always be prepared to give an answer to everyone who asks you to give the reason for the hope that you have" (1 Peter 3:15).

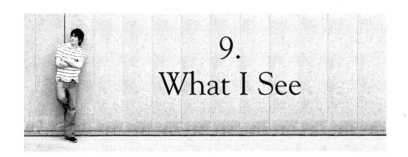

9.
What I See

Often my husband, Ralph, and I discuss over breakfast our latest thoughts on whatever theological inquiry one
of us is into at the moment. A few days ago, we were talking about the subject of this book. Ralph commented that
we parents think the process of raising our kids is supposed
to be a continuum: Mom and Dad train the kids, and the
kids grow year by year, moving on in the path of right-
eousness to live happily ever after. But the idea of this
kind of continuity is false. We have to give kids the permission to wrestle with the cosmic questions. Which
means we have to wrestle with the cosmic questions too.

"Like every living tradition, (Christianity) is
always threatened with the possibility of disintegration,"
writes Lesslie Newbigin. "It has to be sustained in its
integrity by the intellectual vigor and practical courage
with which its members seek to be faithful to it – not by
repeating past formulas but by courageously restating the
tradition in light of new experience." [1] I've tried to present
the new experience that we and our kids are going through
these days. I've tried to pinpoint past formulas that may be
failing us now. And I've tried to add to current discussion

about where we might go from here, sans our past formulas. At the least, I've tried to nudge you to think, and think hard.

Even at this moment, what we're talking about is the world our kids live in right now. Our preschoolers will emerge into their adulthood over a decade from now. What will the world look like then? What challenges will they face? Will you even be here to help them with it?

Here's what I see we need to pursue now for the sake of the newest generation.

1. Strong family mentorship

2. Strong small group mentorship or church mentorship in which at least one (preferably two or more) teacher(s) begins Sunday School with a preschool group and moves with them at every promotion all the way through high school.

3. The realization that at some point children or young adults will (and should) drop the taken-for-grantedness of their faith.

4. The realization that both the strong family and strong church mentorship will be ineffective if the theology is weak or insupportable.

5. The willingness and openess to ask and be asked the hard questions, along with the honesty to wrestle with questions and not give pat answers.

Sound impossible? Ah. That may be the point. John Piper says, "The way God aims to be glorified is by keeping himself in the role of benefactor and keeping us in the role of beneficiaries. He never intends for the patient and the physician to reverse roles. . . . We are still dependent on him to do the humanly impossible in us and through us." [2] Amen.

So what is it kids need to know from us now? That the most important answer is Love. Unconditional, other-centered Love. A Love lavished on them by God. A Love God can pour out through them into the world.

Footnotes and Works Cited

Chapter 1:

1. Dr. Brad Widstrom, The Amazing Race Seminar. Denver. April 2005.
2. Extrapolated from a Barna study, David Kinnamon, director of research. <u>Most Twentysomethings Put Christianity on the Shelf Following Spiritually Active Teen Years.</u> September 11, 2006. "The Barna Update." The Barna Group. 13 September 2007. <http://www.barna.org/FlexPage. aspx?Page=BarnaUpdateandBarnaUpdateID=245>
3. Dick Crider, "Catch 'Em at the Back Door: Ministering to Preteens." Children's Ministry Leadership Conference, Calvary Chapel Conference Center, Murrieta, CA. March 6-8,   2006.
4. Dick Crider.

Chapter 2:

1. The basic stages referred to here are from James W. Fowler, <u>Stages of Faith: The Psychology of Human Development and the Quest for Meaning</u>. (San Francisco: Harper, 1981). To read about each stage in greater detail see Karyn Henley's <u>Child Sensitive Teaching</u>. (Nashville: Child Sensitive Communication, 2002).
2. Lesslie Newbigin, <u>The Gospel in a Pluralist Society</u>. (Grand Rapids: Eerdmans, 1989) 50.
3. Chip Wood, <u>Yardsticks: Children in the Classroom</u>

Ages 4-14. (Greenfield, MA: Northeast Foundation for Children, 1997). This is an excellent look at the stages of development (though not of faith), specifically and practically described according to age.

4. Randall Niles, <u>What Happened to Me? Reflections of a Journey</u>. (New York: iUniverse, 2004) xiii.

5. Chip Wood.

6. Kathryn Tyler, "The Tethered Generation," <u>HR Magazine</u>, May 2007, 42-43.

Chapter 3:

1. James Hall, <u>Philosophy of Religion</u> tape set, lecture 31. (Chantilly, VA: Teaching Company, 2003).

2. Kathryn Tyler, "The Tethered Generation," <u>HR Magazine</u>, May 2007, 45.

3. Mikhail Epstein, <u>The Place of Postmodernism in Postmodernity</u>. 1997 After Postmodernism Conference, nd. <www.focusing.org/apm_papers/epstein.html> 13 September 2007.

4. David Zarefsky, <u>Argumentation: The Study of Effective Reasoning</u> tape set, lecture 7. (Chantilly, VA: Teaching Company, 2001).

5. Robert Solomon, <u>No Excuses: Existentialism and the Meaning of Life</u> tape set, lecture 8. (Chantilly, VA: Teaching Company, 2000).

6. Phillip Carey, <u>Philosophy and Religion in the West</u> tape set, lecture 30. (Chantilly, VA: Teaching Company, 1999).

7. N.T. Wright, <u>Simply Christian</u>. (San Francisco:

HarperCollins, 2006) 43.

8. Lesslie Newbigin, <u>Proper Confidence</u>. (Grand Rapids: Eerdmans, 1995) 83.

9. Kathryn Tyler, "The Tethered Generation," <u>HR Magazine</u>, May 2007, 45.

10. Carl Tinnion, "Postmodernity." Conference, York, England, nd.

11. Carl Tinnion.

Chapter 4

1. Donald Williams, <u>The Great Divide: The Church and the Post-Modernist Challenge</u>. Commencement address, Veritas Christian Academy, June 2, 2001.

2. Flannery O'Connor, <u>Mystery and Manners: Occasional Prose</u>. (New York: Farrar, 1969) 125.

3. Lesslie Newbigin, <u>Proper Confidence</u>. (Grand Rapids: Eerdmans, 1995) 67.

4. Matthew 8:27, NLT

5. Lesslie Newbigin, <u>The Gospel in a Pluralist Society</u>. (Grand Rapids: Eerdmans, 1989) 64.

6. Todd Pruzan, "Global Warning." <u>The New Yorker</u>. 11 April 2005, 34-41.

7. David Zarefsky, <u>Argumentation: The Study of Effective Reasoning</u> tape set, lectures 15 and 16. (Chantilly, VA: Teaching Company, 2001).

8. Ruth A. Tucker, <u>Walking Away from Faith</u>. (Downer's Grove, IL: InterVarsity, 2002) 191.

9. John 17:15, 18, 20, NLT

Chapter 5

1. Julia Cameron, <u>Prayers from a Nonbeliever</u>. (New

York: Tarcher/Putnam, 2003) 1.

2. Ruth A. Tucker, Walking Away from Faith. (Downers Grove, IL: InterVarsity, 2002) 206.

3. Richard Rohr and Andreas Ebert, The Enneagram: A Christian Perspective. (New York: Crossroad, 2001) 21.

4. Donald T. Williams, The Great Divide: The Church and the Post-Modernist Challenge. Commencement address, Veritas Christian Academy, June 2, 2001.

5. Jacob Loewen, "The Shifting God(s) of Western Christianity." Mission Frontiers. May - June 2006, 25-27.

6. N. Kenneth Rideout, The Truth You Know You Know. (Nashville: NDX, 2005) 14.

7. Jacob Loewen.

8. Randall Niles, What Happened to Me? Reflections of a Journey. (New York: iUniverse, 2004) 101, 102.

9. Tim Stafford, Surprised by Jesus. (Downers Grove, IL: InterVarsity, 2006) 34.

10. Rick Chromey, "Smarter Than a Fifth-Grader," Children's Ministry. July/August 2007, 30.

11. Juliet Schor, Born to Buy. (New York: Scribner, 2004) 75.

12. Eric Grimm, "Changing Culture, Changing Stores?" Aspiring Retail. January 2006, 26.

13. Quoted by Michael Larsen, How to Get a Literary Agent. (Naperville, IL: Sourcebooks, 2006) 304.

14. Melinda Henneberger, "Selling Faith," Reader's Digest. August 2005, 180-185.

15. Ladonna Witmer, This Is Who I Am DVD. Producer Bruce Willems. (Elgin, IL: Harbinger, 2006).

16. Tony Lane, "Ministry to Staff's Kids," Children's Ministry, January-February 2006.

17. William Barclay, The Gospel of Matthew, Vol. 2. (Philadelphia: Westminster, 1975) 285.

18. David Kinnamon, director of research. Most Twentysomethings Put Christianity on the Shelf Following Spiritually Active Teen Years. September 11, 2006. "The Barna Update." The Barna Group. 13 September 2007. <http://www.barna.org/FlexPage.aspx?Page=Barna UpdateandBarnaUpdateID=245>

19. N.T. Wright, Simply Christian. (San Francisco: HarperCollins, 2006) 203, 204.

20. Jeremiah 1:10, NIV

Chapter 6
1. N.T. Wright. Evil and the Justice of God. (Downers Grove, IL: InterVarsity, 2006) 76, 102.

2. For a fuller explanation of this apologetic, see Karyn Henley, Love Trumps Karma. (Nashville: Karyn Henley Resources, 2005).

Chapter 7
1. Lesslie Newbigin, The Gospel in a Pluralist Society. (Grand Rapids: Eerdmans, 1989) 242.

2. Peter P. Jacobi, "A Reader's Wish List," The Writer. Aug. 2005, 17-19.

3. Michael Larsen, How to Get a Literary Agent.

(Naperville, IL: Sourcebooks, 2006) 303.
4. Juliet Schor, <u>Born to Buy</u>. (New York: Scribner, 2004) 65.
5. Michael Larsen, 299.

Chapter 8
1. Ben Witherington III, <u>What Have They Done With Jesus?</u> (San Francisco: HarperCollins, 2006) 11.
2. Suzanne Stefanac, <u>Dispatches from Blogistan</u>. (Berkeley: New Riders, 2007) 8.
3. James Hall, <u>Philosophy of Religion</u> tape set, lecture 25. (Chantilly, VA: Teaching Company, 2003).
4. Donald Maass, <u>Writing the Breakout Novel</u>. (Cincinnati: Writer's Digest, 2001) 169.
5. Peter P. Jacobi, "A Reader's Wish List," <u>The Writer</u>. Aug. 2005, 17-19.
6. Lesslie Newbigin, <u>Proper Confidence</u>. (Grand Rapids: Eerdmans, 1995) 75.
7. As Newbigin puts it.
8. For more information about other philosophies and religions and how they compare to Christianity, see Karyn Henley, <u>The Mall of Religions</u>. (Nashville: Karyn Henley Resources, 2007).
9. Lesslie Newbigin, <u>The Gospel in a Pluralist Society</u>. (Grand Rapids: Eerdmans, 1989) 97.
10. Quoted by Ruth A.Tucker, <u>Walking Away from Faith</u>. (Downer's Grove, IL: InterVarsity, 2002) 195.
11. William R. Cook and Ronald B. Herzman, <u>Dante's Divine Comedy</u>, tape set, lecture 24. (Chantilly, VA: Teaching Company, 2001).

12. For a deeper discussion of Truth as Who, see N. Kenneth Rideout, <u>The Truth You Know You Know</u> (Nashville: NDX, 2005).

13. Thomas F.X. Noble, <u>Foundations of Western Civilization</u> tape set, lecture 28. (Chantilly, VA: Teaching Company, 2002).

14. Karyn Henley, <u>If God is Good, Why Do We Suffer?</u> (Nashville: Karyn Henley Resources, 2007). David Marshall, <u>The Truth Behind the New Atheism.</u> (Eugene, OR: Harvest House, 2007).

15. N.T. Wright, <u>Simply Christian</u>. (San Francisco: HarperCollins, 2006) 189-190.

16. Luke Timothy Johnson, <u>The Story of the Bible</u> tape set, lecture 24. (Chantilly, VA: Teaching Company, 2006).

17. Matthew 16:15-17. To read more about the implications of Peter's confession and how the Holy Spirit verifies the truth to the human heart, see <u>The Truth You Know You Know</u> by N. Kenneth Rideout, 100-101.

18. Josh McDowell, <u>New Evidence That Demands a Verdict.</u> (Nashville: Thomas Nelson, 1999) 619.

19. Robert Solomon, <u>Passions: Philosophy and the Intelligence of the Emotions</u> tape set, lecture 17. (Chantilly, VA: Teaching Company, 2006).

20. William Shakespeare. <u>Hamlet</u>, Act 1, scene 4.

21. Quoted by Ruth A.Tucker, <u>Walking Away from Faith</u>. (Downer's Grove, IL: InterVarsity, 2002) 201.

22. William Barclay, <u>The Gospel of Matthew, Vol. 1</u>. (Philadelphia: Westminster, 1975) 389, 390.

23. William Barclay, <u>The Gospel of Mark</u>. (Philadelphia: Westminster, 1975) 25.

24. Tim Stafford, <u>Surprised by Jesus</u>. (Downers Grove, IL: InterVarsity, 2006) 99.

Chapter 9
1. Lesslie Newbigin, <u>The Gospel in a Pluralist Society</u>. (Grand Rapids: Eerdmans, 1989) 63.
2. John Piper, <u>Desiring God</u>. (Sisters, OR: Multomah, 1996) 206.